Corgi Toys
The Ones With Windows

James Wieland

Dr. Edward Force

Photographs by Thomas Budney of Bantam, Connecticut

Motorbooks International
Publishers & Wholesalers Inc.
Osceola, Wisconsin 54020, USA

© 1981 by James Wieland and Edward Force
ISBN: 0-87938-123-X
Library of Congress Number 80-27782

Printed and bound in the United States of America.

Book and cover design by William F. Kosfeld

10 9 8 7 6 5 4 3 2

Motorbooks International books are also available at discounts in
bulk quantity for industrial or sales-promotional use. For details
write to Marketing Manager, Motorbooks International, 729
Prospect Avenue, P.O. Box 2, Osceola, Wisconsin, 54020, USA.

Library of Congress Cataloging in Publication Data

Wieland, James, 1946-
  Corgi toys.

  1. Corgi toys. I. Force, Edward, 1938-   joint
author. II. Title.
TL237.W53   688.7'2   80-27782
ISBN 0-87938-123-X (pbk.)

CONTENTS

INTRODUCTION

In 1956 the firm of Playcraft Toys introduced their first Corgi miniature vehicles. They had made such toys before, under the name of Mettoy, but these were few in number and their quality could not compare with that of Dinky Toys and other diecast cars then on the market. The Corgi line took its name from a Welsh breed of dog because the Playcraft and Mettoy factories (the two were sister corporations then, and have since merged) were located in Swansea, South Wales. From the start, Corgi Toys were intended to be not only competitive, but superior to the competition, and the competition consisted mainly of Dinky Toys.

In those days most miniature cars consisted of a zamak (zinc alloy) body casting, a baseplate, usually of sheet metal, and the usual axles, wheels and tires. From the start Corgi cars had all of that, plus the feature that was stressed in the firm's early advertising: clear plastic windows to make the cars more realistic. In addition, the first Corgi cars were issued in two forms: one conventional, the other with a push-and-go flywheel motor. These 'mechanical' Corgis were not a great success and were phased out in 1959; but the windows, followed by a long line of other features (which some collectors, to be sure, refer to as gimmicks), thrust the Corgi line into instant competition with Dinky Toys, and inevitably caused similar efforts by the miniature car industry in general and Meccano, Ltd., the makers of Dinky Toys, in particular.

Like the Dinky Toys of the time, the first Corgis were made to approximately 1/45 to 1/48 scale. When large commercial vehicles were introduced, they were made to somewhat smaller scales so as not to be too much bigger than the cars. These Corgi Majors, as the larger vehicles have been known ever since, were introduced in 1957. Practically every year thereafter saw the birth of something new and different in the Corgi line: in 1958, the first Royal Air Force (RAF) vehicles; in 1959, spring suspension and detailed interiors; in 1960, loads of bricks, sacks, planks and milk churns cast in blocks to fit into the model trucks; in 1961, jeweled headlights, opening hoods, detailed engines beneath those hoods, window blinds and contoured wheel hubs more realistic than the plain hubs used until then; in 1962, more opening parts plus fingertip steering and Trans-o-lite optic fiber lights; in 1963, swiveling headlights; in 1964, working windshield wipers and steering by means of a turning roof sign; in 1965, the introduction of a single model (the James Bond Aston Martin) so filled with special features that it took the toy industry by storm. And so the process has continued to the present. Not all Corgi innovations have been successful (the Golden Jacks of 1968 were the firm's outstanding failure), but the Corgi policy of constant innovation has made the firm a leader in the field in terms of its effect on the industry and, even more important, on sales of the products.

Corgi's flexible approach to the scale of its products continued until 1967, when, along with Dinky, the models began to appear in a slightly larger scale of approximately 1/43. This was a minor change, unlike that which began in 1972, when, again paralleling a similar change in Dinky Toys, a 1/36 scale was introduced. This change to substantially larger models may have provided children with more play value—not to mention sturdiness. It did not, however, please the majority of collectors, into whose collections of more-or-less 1/43 scale models the new Corgis did not fit smoothly at all. The decrease in collector interest may have had something to do with the firm's most noticeable trend since then: toward producing more and more products that are not models of real cars and trucks, but rather representations of vehicles from comic strips, movies and television shows. Such toys have, if anything, turned off collector interest all the more, but the fact that Corgi produces more and more of them must indicate that they sell well.

And so the story of Corgi Toys continues. Having enjoyed more than twenty-five good years, the firm can look forward to continued success in a field in which all too many firms have gone out of business in recent years. For most collectors, though, it is the earlier Corgis of the pre-1/36 scale era that are most interesting, and we shall stress them as they deserve to be stressed, and make this book a complete history of Corgi Toys's first twenty-five years.

1956: THE ONES WITH WINDOWS

Except for two sports cars and two trucks, which simply didn't have room for the flywheel motor, every one of the first Corgi Toys was produced in both regular and mechanical form, with an M added to the catalog number to denote the latter type. All of them featured clear plastic windows, or at least windshields in the case of the two open sports cars, and all had treaded rubber tires on plain metal hubs. Some baseplates were of pressed steel, soon to be phased out; others were of diecast metal, indicating the more realistic type of base that was to prevail. Many models were produced in a variety of solid-color and two-tone finishes. The 1956 Corgi Toys were:

200: Ford Consul, 90 mm long, a typical British family car, available in cream, tan, gray, green and cream, gray and green or two-tone green; produced through 1961.
200M: the mechanical version, in blue or dark green; issued through 1959.

201: Austin Cambridge A50, 90 mm, as common as the Consul, in cream, gray, turquoise, two-tone green or green and silver; issued through 1960.
201M: mechanical, in orange, gray or cream; through 1959.

202: Morris Cowley, 91 mm, another of the genre, in blue, gray, green, gray and blue or blue and white; through 1960.
202M: mechanical, in green or greenish off-white; through 1959.

203: Vauxhall Velox, 91 mm, yet another typical British car, in red, cream, yellow or red and cream; through 1960.
203M: mechanical, in red or yellow; through 1959.

204: Rover 90, 97 mm, a larger but equally typical car, in off-white, light or dark gray, maroon and gray or bronze and red; through 1960.
204M: mechanical, in green or gray; through 1959.

205: Riley Pathfinder, 97 mm, handsomest of the family, in red or blue; through 1961.
205M: mechanical, in red or blue; through 1959.

206: Hillman Husky, 86 mm, a small station wagon, in solid tan or blue and silver; through 1960.
206M: mechanical, in cream, light gray or dark blue; through 1959.

300: Austin-Healey 100-4, 86 mm, one of Britain's best-known open sports cars of the time, in red with cream interior or cream with red, featuring clear plastic windshield, detailed interior and diecast steering wheel; through 1963.

301: Triumph TR2, 86 mm, slimmer and higher than the Austin-Healey, with the same features, in cream or light green; through 1959, when the TR3 replaced it.

403: Bedford 15 cwt Daily Express van, 83 mm, one of numerous uses of the Bedford casting, in blue with "Daily Express" decals; through 1961.

403M: mechanical, in red with "K.L.G." decals; through 1959. (The KLG firm, founded by old-time racing driver Kenelm Lee Guinness, makes spark plugs, and the Daily Express, one of Britain's most popular newspapers, sponsors the International Trophy auto race.)

404: Bedford Dormobile, 83 mm, the 16 cwt with full side windows making it a minibus, in cream, green, turquoise, dark red, yellow and blue or two-tone blue; through 1962.
404M: mechanical, in metallic red or turquoise, through 1959.

405: Bedford Utilicar Fire Tender, 83 mm, with a ladder on its roof, in green with "Auxiliary Fire Service" decals, later in red with "Fire Department" decals; through 1961, revised into number 423 in 1960.
405M: mechanical, in red with "Fire Department" decals; through 1959.

452: Commer 5-Ton Dropside Truck, 120 mm, with separate chassis-cab and low-side open rear body castings, the former red or blue, the latter cream; through 1963.

453: Commer 5-Ton Refrigerator Truck Van, 117 mm, the same chassis-cab in light or dark blue with a cream rear box body and red-white-blue "Wall's Ice Cream" decals; through 1960.

1957: THE FAMILY GROWS

To the original Corgi series of cars (200's), sports cars (300's) and commercial vehicles (400's) were added trailers (100's), racing cars (150's), Corgi Majors (1100's) and gift sets (single numbers, later to run through number 49). Thus, by 1957, the basis of Corgi numbering was established, with only farm machinery (50's) and various specialized series (500's through 900's) to come later. The 1957 issues included:

100: Dropside Trailer, 108 mm, the rear body casting of the 452 truck, plus a chassis, four wheels and a wire towbar, in red and cream, blue and red, or cream and white; through 1964.

150: Vanwall Formula I Racing Car, 91 mm, the car that won the World Championship for its manufacturers the following year, in a lighter green than the real car, with clear plastic windshield, tan seat, name and number decals; renumbered 150S in 1961 when suspension was added, and produced in that form through 1965.

207: Standard Vanguard, 95 mm, another typical British sedan, in two-tone finish with white, light green or light gray paired with red; through 1962. **207M:** mechanical, in light green and red or solid yellow; through 1959.

302: MGA, 90 mm, a good-looking and very popular sports car with detailed open interior, steering wheel and windshield, in red and cream, green and cream or white and red; through 1965.

406: Land Rover Open Pickup, 95 mm, first of many Corgi Land Rover variations, in yellow and black or blue and cream (the second color that of the roof); through 1962.

407: Smiths Karrier Bantam Mobile Grocery Shop, 93 mm, another versatile vehicle, in pale green with "Home Services" decals and groceries in its windows; through 1961.

408: Bedford 15 cwt Van, 83 mm, this time in AA (Automobile Association) yellow and black as a road service vehicle, as its roof sign and side decals proclaim; through 1962.

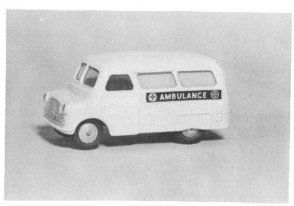

412: Bedford 15 cwt Utilicar Ambulance, the same casting in cream, with "Ambulance" decals and opaque rear windows; through 1960.

413: Smiths Karrier Bantam Butcher Shop, 93 mm, in white and blue, with appropriate decals and meaty window displays, otherwise the same as 407; through 1962.

454: Commer 5-Ton Platform Truck, 120 mm, the usual Commer chassis-cab unit in blue or yellow with a gray rear bed; through 1962.

1101: Bedford Carrimore Car Transporter, 263 mm, the first Corgi Major, with red cab, blue semi-trailer and light green upper deck; replaced by 1105 (with a newer cab) in 1962.
GS 1: the first Corgi Gift Set, consisting of the 1101 Car Transporter with a full load of four cars: British cars at first, American in 1959, and assorted newer issues in 1962, its last year.

208: Jaguar 2.4-Liter, 95 mm, sleek and stately, in white; modified to 208S in 1960 and produced in that form through 1963.
208M: mechanical, in metallic dark blue; through 1959.

210: Citroen DS19, 97 mm, Corgi's first foreign car, in red and yellow or green and black; upgraded to 210S in 1960 and surviving thus through 1965.

455: Karrier Bantam 2-Ton Van, 102 mm, possibly the only Corgi based directly on an earlier Mettoy, with a single casting including cab, chassis, rear roof and solid ends, in blue, and a red baseplate casting supplying the rear bed (the sides are completely open); through 1960. The cab is similar but not identical to that of the 407 and 413 mobile shops.

1958: ROCKETS AND MISSILES
AND RAF BLUE

The major addition to the Corgi line in 1958 was a group of military models, some in army olive drab, others in the dull blue of the Royal Air Force. All the Corgi series were added to, the year's new issues being:

101: Platform Trailer, 108 mm, made from the flatbed casting of 454, in red and blue, yellow and blue, yellow and gray, blue and gray, and all yellow; through 1962.

102: Rice 1-Horse Pony Trailer, 86 mm, with lowering tailgate and plastic occupant, in red and black, ivory and red, and two combinations of tan and cream; through 1965.

151: Lotus Eleven, 83 mm, in silver or dull blue, a low, wide small-displacement sports-racing car with windshield, steering wheel, red seats, and number decals; updated to 151S in 1961 and made through 1964.

152: BRM Formula I Racing Car, 91 mm, a little too light to be authentic but more nearly so than the pale green 152S issued from 1961 through 1965. Windshield, number decal, unpainted seat and steering wheel.

209: Riley Pathfinder Police Car, 97 mm, the 205 casting with roof sign, antenna and black paint; through 1961.

350: Thunderbird Guided Missile on Towing Trolley, 140 mm, with silver or ice blue rocket and red rubber nose cone, the trolley in RAF blue; through 1962.

351: RAF Land Rover, 95 mm, the 406 casting in blue with a tinplate rear cover, handy for towing 350; made through 1963—a 351S version was shown in the 1962 Corgi catalog but never produced.

352: Standard Vanguard RAF Staff Car, 95 mm, 207 in blue with number and rondel decal; through 1961.

411: Karrier Bantam Lucozade Van, 102 mm, a variation on the 455 theme, being a single casting including cab and box body, with a raising plastic door on the left side, in yellow (except for the gray sliding door), with "Lucozade" labels; through 1962, also used as the 435 Dairy Van in 1962.

457: ERF 44G Platform Truck, 120 mm, a new chassis-cab casting with the flatbed from the Commer 454, in light blue with darker blue flatbed; through 1962.

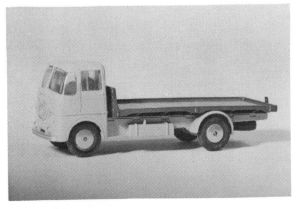

458: ERF 64G Earth Dumper, 95 mm, an almost identical cab with shorter chassis in red plus a dark yellow tipper; through 1967.

1100: Bedford Carrimore Low Loader No. 1, 220 mm, with red or yellow cab and dark blue semi-trailer with low sides and silver winch; through 1963.

1102: Euclid Bulldozer, 159 mm, a massive machine in lime green or yellow with silver blade on two hydraulic arms, two black stacks and black rubber treads; replaced by 1107 in 1962.

1104: Bedford Carrimore Low Loader No. 2 Machinery Carrier, 220 mm, the cab from 1100 in red and a flat silver-gray semi-trailer with detachable rear wheels; through 1962. It lacks the low sides and tailgate of the No. 1 type (1100), but has the winch.

1115: Bristol-Ferranti Blood-hound Guided Missile, white and yellow or all white with red nose cone; available separately through 1960.

GS 4: RAF Land Rover, Blood-hound Missile, Platform and Trolley (351, 1115, 1116 and 1117), despite the mixture of olive drab and RAF blue; through 1961.

211: 1957 Studebaker Golden Hawk, 104 mm, Corgi's first model of an American car, and still a favorite of American collectors, in blue with gold trim; upgraded to 211S in 1960 and produced as such through 1965.
211M: mechanical, in white with gold trim; through 1959.

303: Mercedes-Benz 300SL Convertible, 95 mm, in blue and yellow, blue and white or white and blue, the second color being that of the interior, and equipped with windshield and steering wheel; updated to 303S in 1961 and produced through 1966.

459: ERF 44G Moorhouse Van, 117 mm, the 457 chassis-cab in yellow with a red rear box, "Moorhouses Jam" and "Moorhouses Lemon Cheese" decals on the two sides; through 1960.

1116: Bristol-Ferranti Missile Launching Ramp, olive and cream, through 1960.

1108: Bloodhound Missile on Platform, 178 mm, a combination of 1115 and 1116; through 1961.

1117: Bristol-Ferranti Missile Trolley, olive drab; through 1960.

1109: Bloodhound Missile on Trolley, 228 mm, 1115 and 1117 combined; through 1962.

1401: Service Ramp, 151 mm, a garage lift in blue and white; made through 1960. One of Corgi's many accessories.

GS 2: Land Rover and Pony Trailer, a plastic-covered version of 406, replaced in 1963 by 438, pulling the 102 Pony Trailer; through 1968.

GS 3: RAF Land Rover and Thunderbird on Trolley, a natural combination of 351 and 350; through 1963.

1959: SUSPENSION SPRINGS UP

The big news from Corgi in 1959 was the addition of spring suspension to a few cars. The use of suspension grew, of course, with other early models converted during the next two years, by which time suspension on new Corgis was taken for granted. As suspension was being introduced, the mechanical models were being discontinued; two new mechanical models were issued in 1959, but at the year's end all the mechanicals were deleted. The 1959 issues included Corgi's first agricultural models, plus two unusual radar scanners, in addition to a number of more typical items, among them closed cars with detailed plastic interiors. The new issues were:

50: Massey-Ferguson 65 Farm Tractor, 79 mm, in red and cream or red and gray, with steering wheel, trailer hitch and detailed engine; through 1966.

51: Tipping Farm Trailer, 102 mm, in red and yellow or red and gray, with tipping action and a lowering tailgate; through 1965.

216: Austin A40, 86 mm, a boxy British compact car, in two-tone blue; through 1962.
216M: mechanical, in red and black, issued only in 1959.

219: 1959 Plymouth Sports Suburban, 104 mm, a typical American station wagon in cream and tan, replaced by a newer version in 1963. It has a red plastic interior, sharing with the next two models the honor of being the first Corgi closed cars so equipped.

222: Renault Floride, 91 mm, with cream or red plastic interior. It was issued briefly in dark red without suspension, then in dark red, blue or light green with suspension, but without an S added to its number; through 1965.

223: Chevrolet Impala State Patrol Car, 108 mm, a rare case of a specialized version being issued before the generic type, in black with white "State Patrol" decals on the doors, gray antenna and yellow interior; replaced by 481 in 1965.

353: Decca Radar Scanner, 83 mm high, not a vehicle but a stationary piece of airfield equipment, with RAF blue base, orange and silver scanner; through 1960.

409: Jeep FC-150 Pickup Truck, 91 mm, light blue with red grille; through 1965.

416: Royal Auto Club Land Rover, 95 mm, the 406 casting in RAC medium blue, with tin rear cover, antenna, roof sign and decals; updated to 416S in 1962 and issued thus through 1964.

460: ERF Neville Cement Truck, 95 mm, with the 64G short-chassis cab unit in yellow and a silver tipper unit with cover, tailgate, two red caps on top and a "Tunnel Cement" decal between them; through 1966.

1106: Decca Airfield Radar Truck, 134 mm, a Karrier Gamecock cab in yellow with yellow and orange striped house to which the scanner from 353 and an antenna are attached. A cogwheel on the left side allows the scanner to be turned. Like 353, it was made only through 1960; I suspect neither sold well.

1110: Bedford Articulated Tanker, 191 mm, the usual cab unit with a tanker semi-trailer, both in red, with blue and white "Mobilgas" decals; issued through 1965, replaced by a newer version the following year.

1111: Massey-Ferguson 700 Combine Harvester, 172 mm, a massive thing in red with various yellow bits and heavy black tires on yellow wheels; issued through 1963. A second version, using the same number but equipped with plastic tines and other parts in place of the original metal, was issued in 1969.

1112: Corporal Guided Missile on Ramp, 330 mm high, with white and red missile and olive ramp; through 1962. **1124: Corporal Missile Ramp**; issued separately in either 1960 or '61, only for about a year.

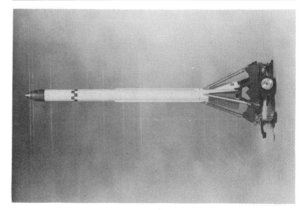

1113: Corporal Guided Missile on Erector Truck, 292 mm, the same missile as 1112 whose trolley is attached to a long split-cab olive truck from which it raises to a vertical position; through 1962.

GS 9: The Corporal Missile, Ramp, Erector and 6x6 Army Truck (1112, 1113 and 1118); through 1962.

213: Jaguar 2.4-Liter Fire Service Car, 95 mm, the 208 casting in red with roof sign, antenna and fire service emblem decals; updated to 213S in 1961 and produced through 1962.

214: 1959 Ford Thunderbird Hardtop, 102 mm, in light green with cream top, a very popular model, almost petite though it represents a big sports car; updated to 214S in 1962 and produced through 1965.
214M: mechanical, in light green and white or pink and black; issued only in 1959.

215: 1959 Ford Thunderbird Convertible, 102 mm, the open version of the same car, with the usual open-car features, in white with blue interior; also upgraded in 1962 and made through 1965, and equally popular today.

304: Mercedes-Benz 300SL Coupe, 95 mm, companion to 303, though not as pretty, in yellow with red roof or all yellow; updated to 304S in 1961 and made through 1966.

1118: International 6x6 Covered Army Truck, 140 mm, in olive including its removable metal cover; through 1963, when it became the 1133 Troop Transporter.

GS 7: The Farm Tractor and Trailer (50 and 51); through 1963, replaced by number 29.

GS 8: The Farm Tractor and Trailer plus the 1111 Combine; through 1962.

1960: TO THE CIRCUS BY HOVERCRAFT

The 1960 Corgis included a number of interesting and popular models, from a Mini and a Bluebird speed record car to a hovercraft and a circus set, plus several accessories and an increased use of suspension and detailed car interiors. The new issues were:

53: Massey-Ferguson 65 Tractor with Shovel, 124 mm, the 50 Tractor equipped with a shovel loader, in red and cream or red and gray, the second color including the arms while the shovel was unpainted; through 1967.

153: Bluebird Speed Record Car, 127 mm, in blue with varying decals and wheels—first metal wheels with tires, later one-piece black plastic wheels; updated to 153A in 1963, made as such through 1965 and highly prized today.

208S: Jaguar 2.4 with suspension and interior, in light yellow; through 1963.

210S: Citroen DS19 with suspension and interior, in red or yellow; through 1965.

211S: 1957 Studebaker Golden Hawk, similarly updated, in gold with white trim; through 1966.

217: Fiat 1800 Sedan (left), 95 mm, in mustard yellow, light blue, two-tone blue or cream and brown, with interior and suspension; issued through 1962 and reappearing with slight changes as the 232 Fiat 2100 (right) in 1961.

218: Aston Martin DB4, 95 mm, a lovely fastback in red or yellow, with suspension and interior; made through 1965 and offered in competition form in 1962 as 309.

220: 1959 Chevrolet Impala 4-Door Hardtop, already seen in State Patrol form in 1959, now in civilian pink, tan or light blue, 108 mm long, issued in this form through 1965 and replaced by a newer form, 248, that year.

221: 1959 Impala Taxi, 108 mm, the same casting in yellow with taxi sign, antenna and decals; replaced in 1965. All the Impalas had interiors and suspension.

226: Morris Mini-Minor (right), 73 mm, in light blue, later in metallic maroon, with interior and suspension as was customary by now; this very popular little car was the first of a long line of Corgi Minis and remained in production through 1971. **225: Austin Seven Mini (left),** 73 mm, a playmate for 226, in red; first issued in 1961 and ran through 1966 or '67.

305: Triumph TR3, 86 mm, in light green or cream, replacing the earlier TR2; it was updated to 305S in 1962 and produced as such through 1964.

417: Land Rover Breakdown Tow Truck, 114 mm, in red with yellow top, unpainted crane, roof light and decals; after being updated to 417S in 1962, receiving a plastic top to replace the original tinplate one, it lasted through 1965.

418: Austin Taxi, 97 mm, the typical black London taxi with orange taxi sign and yellow interior; through 1974, a tribute to its popularity.

419: Ford Zephyr Motorway Police Patrol Car, 97 mm, a white station wagon with antenna, dome light and decals; issued through 1965, with its civilian counterpart appearing as 424 in 1961—again the police version appears before the civilian type.

421: Bedford Evening Standard Van, 83 mm, the familiar Bedford 12 cwt in black and silver plus decals; through 1962.

422: Bedford Corgi Toys Van, 83 mm, another variation on the same theme, in the Corgi colors of blue and yellow plus decals; through 1962.

423: Bedford Fire Department Van, 82 mm, a revision of 405, in red with ladder and decals; through 1962.

456: ERF Dropside Truck, 120 mm, the long-chassis 44G cab in yellow with dark blue low-side rear as used on 100 and 452; through 1963.

1103: Euclid TC12 Tractor, 120 mm, in lime green with dark bluish-green motor and black or white treads, the 1102 casting without its bulldozer blade; through 1964.

1119: HDL SR-N1 Hovercraft, 120 mm, a new departure for Corgi, with metallic silver-gray body, dark blue motor housing and white air intake; through 1962.

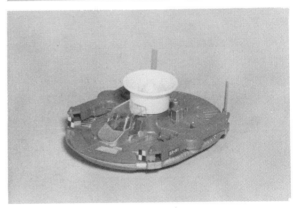

1121: International 6x6 Circus Crane Truck, 200 mm, the first of Corgi's Chipperfields Circus models, in red with yellow crane and blue lettering, through 1968.

1485, 1486 and 1488: Loads of Bricks, Planks and Sacks, and Milk Churns made to fit into the Commer and ERF trucks.

1490: Skip with Milk Churns, a sort of rear shelf for attachment to a tractor. Not many seem to have been sold, and some people doubt this item's existence.

GS 11: ERF Dropside Truck and Platform Trailer (456 and 101), with Loads of Bricks, Planks and Sacks (1485 and 1486), in yellow and blue; through 1964.

GS 12: Circus Crane Truck and Cage Trailer, 1121 and what was issued separately the next year as 1123, in Chipperfields red and blue; through 1965.

1961: JEWELED HEADLIGHTS, CONTOURED WHEELS AND WINDOW BLINDS

Corgi's plain wheel hubs were replaced in 1961 by more realistic contoured hubs, and the headlights that were just silvered blobs integral with the body began to give way to jeweled separate pieces. Engine hoods that opened, with detailed motors beneath them, chrome-plated bumpers and grilles, and even Venetian blinds were among Corgi's 1961 strivings for greater realism. More and more models were fitted with suspension and plastic interiors, and a series of accessory kits joined the Corgi family so that realistic settings for the cars could be set up. The year's new issues were:

55: Fordson Power Major Tractor, 83 mm, in light blue with orange wheels, featuring a vibrating exhaust stack—which Märklin had introduced years before; through 1963.

152S: BRM with suspension, driver and Union Jack decal, in pale green with silver trim; through 1965.

213S: Jaguar 2.4-Liter Fire Service Car with suspension and interior, red as usual; through 1962.

224: Bentley Continental Sports Saloon, 108 mm, a fine model in silver gray and black, two-tone green, or gold (the last from a gift set), with jeweled headlights and chrome-plated grille and bumpers; through 1966.

229: 1960 Chevrolet Corvair 700, 97 mm, in light blue, darker blue or gold (from a gift set), with rear window blind, opening rear hood and engine detail; through 1966.

231: Triumph Herald Coupe, 90 mm, in light blue and white or gold and white, with the entire front body opening to give access to the detailed engine; through 1966. Dinky did a very similar model, also in light blue and white, but without the opening front.

234: Ford Consul Classic 315, 95 mm, in tan with pink roof or (in that same gift set) gold, with opening hood and detailed engine; through 1965.

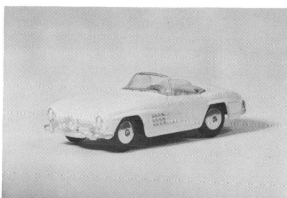

303S: Mercedes-Benz 300SL Roadster with suspension, in white, blue or gold with racing number and stripes; through 1966.

304S: Mercedes-Benz 300SL Coupe with suspension, in silver and red or white and red, with number and stripe decals; through 1966.

414: Bedford Army Ambulance, 83 mm, the familiar 15 cwt van in olive with decals and opaque rear windows; through 1963.

424: Ford Zephyr Estate Car, 97 mm, already out in police form, now civilian in two-tone blue with the same red interior as the police car; through 1965.

1120: Midland Red Express Coach, 140 mm, a singledeck bus in red and black with interior and decals; through 1963. Despite the popularity of model buses, this model did not sell well and is quite a rarity today.

1123: Circus Cage Wagon, already seen a year earlier in a gift set, in the red, blue and tan of Chipperfields, a 127 mm four-wheeled wagon with animals in its cages; through 1963.

1126: Ecurie Ecosse Racing Car Transporter, 197 mm, a very popular model of an equally popular racing team's vehicle, in the dark blue of Ecurie Ecosse, later in a lighter shade; through 1965. Too bad Corgi never made a D-Type Jaguar to go with it, as the team, run by Scotsman David Murray, was best known for its 1956 and '57 Le Mans victories in D-Types.

56: Four Furrow Plough, 90 mm, with red frame and yellow blades; through 1963.

150S: Vanwall with suspension, painted red—heaven knows why!—with blue and white stripes, number 25 and driver; through 1965.

151S: Lotus Eleven with suspension and driver, similarly brightened in blue and silver; through 1964.

232: Fiat 2100, the 217 Fiat 1800 warmed over, with two-tone purple paint, jeweled head-lights and rear window blind; through 1964.

601 through 607: building kits and other accessories: 601 Batley Garage, 602AA and RAC Phone Boxes, 603 Silverstone Racing Pits, 604 Silverstone Press Box, 605 Silverstone Club House, 606 Lampposts and 607 Elephant in Cage. All were made through 1968, with 601 in production one year longer.

GS 14: Jeep FC-150 with overhead service tower, lamppost and workman; through 1965, re-issued that year as 478 without the lamppost (which was 606), but with the workman with upraised arms.

GS 15: Silverstone Racing Layout, with varying components including 150, 151, 152, 215, 304, 309, 417, the three Silverstone buildings, etc.; through 1966.

GS 16: Ecurie Ecosse Transporter (1126) with Vanwall, Lotus and BRM (150, 151 and 152); through 1966. (I must confess I painted three Dinky D-Jags dark blue and put them in mine.)

GS 18: Fordson Tractor and Plough (55 and 56); through 1963.

GS 20: Golden Guinea Set, with gold-plated 224 Bentley, 229 Corvair and 234 Ford Consul, and selling for a guinea (21 shillings); it may not have been issued until 1963, but it was not on the market long and is a rarity today.

1962: OPENING TRUNKS
AND FRINGED UMBRELLAS

The Corgi innovations continued in 1962, with opening trunks joining the hoods of 1961, battery operated lights appearing on the new ambulance, and an interesting novelty in the form of a Bermuda Taxi with fringed umbrella. The new models were:

54: Fordson Tractor with Half-tracks, 91 mm, the 55 Tractor with dual rear wheels carrying rubber treads, in the usual blue finish; through 1964.

214S: 1959 Ford Thunderbird Coupe, with suspension and interior, in metallic gray with red top; through 1965.

215S: 1959 Ford Thunderbird Convertible, with suspension and driver, in red and yellow; through 1965.

227: BMC Morris Mini-Cooper Competition Car, 73 mm, the Mini casting in light blue and white or yellow and white, with crossed flags and racing number decals; through 1965.

228: Volvo P-1800 Coupe, 95 mm, in tan, red, pink or dark orange, with red or yellow interior; through 1965.

233: Trojan-Heinkel Bubblecar, 64 mm, even smaller than the Mini, in red, pink, orange, lilac or metallic dark blue; through 1972.

235: 1961 Oldsmobile 88, 108 mm, a typical American sedan—the Canadian version, in fact—in light or metallic blue and white or solid metallic blue; through 1966.

237: 1961 Oldsmobile Sheriff's Car, 108 mm, in black and white, with red dome light and huge "County Sheriff" labels; same casting as 235; made through 1966.

238: Jaguar Mark X Saloon, 108 mm, in silver, orange-red, light blue, metallic blue or green, with opening hood and trunk, engine details, luggage and jeweled headlights; through 1967.

307: Jaguar E-Type, 95 mm, in dark red or dark metallic gray with red removable hardtop and tan interior, a lovely and popular model; issued through 1964 and reappearing that year in competition form as 312.

309: Aston Martin Competition, 95 mm, the 218 DB4 in green and white with crossed flags and racing numbers; through 1965.

420: Ford Thames Airborne Caravan, 95 mm, a raised-roof home on wheels, in off-white and light green, lilac and purple or light and medium blue, with opening rear doors and detailed interior; shown in the 1961 catalog but apparently issued from 1962 through 1967.

426: Karrier Circus Booking Office, 91 mm, the Bantam mobile shop in Chipperfields red and blue, with decals; through 1964—a very rare and desired model today.

430: 1959 Ford Thunderbird Bermuda Taxi, 102 mm, an interesting novelty in white with bright-colored green, yellow or blue rectangular plastic umbrella with red fringe over the otherwise open interior, driver in shirt and shorts, and decals; issued through 1965 and quite a collector's item now. Oddly enough, the real thing was an impossibility, as Bermuda then allowed only cars with engines up to 1500 cc.

431: Volkswagen Pickup Truck, 91 mm, in yellow with red detachable plastic top; through 1966. One source lists it as having been issued in 1964.

433: Volkswagen Delivery Van, 91 mm, in red and white; through 1964.

434: Volkswagen Kombi, 91 mm, the bus version of the van, in two-tone light green; through 1966.

435: Commer Dairy Milk Van, 102 mm, the 411 casting in light blue and white with sliding yellow plastic side door and "Drive Safely on Milk" decals; through 1963.

436: Citroen Safari ID19, 108 mm, a dark yellow station wagon with opening tailgate, folding rear seats, green or brown luggage on roof rack and "Wildlife Preservation" decals; through 1965. Possibly not issued until 1963.

437: 1962 Cadillac Superior Ambulance, 114 mm, in red and cream or blue and white, with battery-operated roof lights; through 1968.

438: Covered Land Rover, 95 mm, a long-wheelbase replacement for 406, in green (various shades) or tan with cream, gray or olive plastic cover on the back, this handy vehicle was produced through 1977.

1105: Bedford Carrimore Car Transporter, 263 mm, red and two-tone blue, with a new-type Bedford cab, replacing 1101; through 1966.

1129: Bedford Milk Tanker, 191 mm, a blue and white version of 1110, with "Milk" logo; through 1965, replaced in 1966 by 1141.

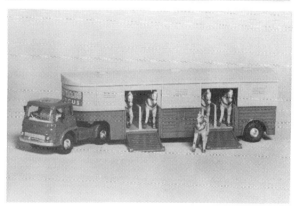

1130: Bedford Circus Horse Transporter, 260 mm, in Chipperfields red and blue, with opening doors that become ramps for six plastic horses; through 1971.

GS 19: Circus Land Rover (a version of 438 not issued separately), with red and blue 101 Flat Trailer carrying the 607 Elephant Cage; through 1969.

230: Mercedes-Benz 220SE Coupe, 102 mm, in cream, dark red or black, with opening trunk, spare wheel and "Authentic self-centering steering;" through 1964, when it was replaced by the 253 version.

305S: Triumph TR3 with suspension, in metallic light green as usual; through 1964.

416S: Land Rover with suspension and plastic top, still in its blue RAC finish; through 1964.

417S: Land Rover Breakdown Tow Truck, still red and yellow but with suspension and minor revisions; through 1965, replaced then by 477.

608 through 611: more plastic items: 608 Shell or B. P. Service Station, 609 Accessories for 608, 610 Police Box and Phone Box, and 611 Chalet (or Motel Cabin); all issued through 1968.

1107: Euclid TC12 Bulldozer, 159 mm, in lime green or red, an updated replacement for the earlier 1102; through 1966.

1963: THE JOLLY, THE STING RAY AND TRANS-O-LITE

Corgi's 1963 products included a second umbrellaed open car, the Fiat Jolly, and an exciting Corvette Sting Ray with swiveling headlights. Many models appeared with the now-common opening doors or hoods, and one had an opening rear window, while an ice cream van included sliding windows and a swiveling vendor inside. But the most striking innovation was Trans-o-lite, an optic fiber system in which a panel somewhere on the vehicle picked up light and carried it to the headlights or taillights—or, in one later model, both. Issued in 1963 were:

57: Massey-Ferguson Tractor with Fork Loader, 127 mm, in red and either cream or gray, with an unpainted fork replacing the shovel of 53; through 1967.

154: 1961 Ferrari Formula I, 91 mm, a good model of the 1961 World Championship car in red, with driver, chromed engine and exhausts, and Ferrari emblem and number decals. A very popular item, it remained in production through 1971.

239: VW 1500 Karmann-Ghia Coupe, 91 mm, in light red, cream or gold, with opening front and rear hoods, engine detail, luggage and spare wheel; through 1968.

240: Ghia-Fiat 600 Jolly, 79 mm, a canopied beach car in light or dark blue with chrome trim and two figures; revised as 242 in 1965.

241: Chrysler Ghia L64, 108 mm, in metallic blue, green or gold, with opening doors, hood and trunk, interior with detailed dashboard and rear-view mirror, and even a Corgi dog on the rear shelf; through 1969.

251: Hillman Imp, 83 mm, light or dark metallic blue or golden bronze, with an opening rear window, much like a present-day hatchback; through 1967.

252: Rover 2000, 95 mm, in blue or maroon, with Trans-o-lite headlights whose light comes through the rear defogger panel; through 1966.

310: 1963 Corvette Sting Ray, 90 mm, a big hit in metallic dark red, silver or copper, with jeweled headlights that swivel open and shut, chrome-plated trim and spoked wheels; produced through 1968 and highly prized today.

316: N.S.U. Sport Prinz, 86 mm, a jaunty little sport coupe in metallic dark red; through 1966.

428: Mister Softee Ice Cream Van, 91 mm, a light blue and cream Karrier of bulbous proportions, with sliding side windows, plus a vendor inside who can be turned to face in any direction; through 1966.

439: 1959 Chevrolet Impala Fire Chief, 108 mm, the usual Chevy casting in solid red or red and white, with dome light, antenna, decals and two figures inside; replaced by 428 in 1965.

441: Volkswagen Toblerone Van, 91 mm, a blue version of 433 with "Chocolate Tobler" decals and Trans-o-lite headlights, their light supplied by a roof panel; through 1967 and very popular today.

443: 1959 Plymouth Suburban US Mail Car, 104 mm, a new version of 219 in blue and white postal livery, with decals and red stripes; through 1966.
445. 1959 Plymouth Suburban, 104 mm, the civilian version in light blue and red; through 1965.

464: Commer 15 cwt Police Van, 90 mm, introducing an often-used new light van, in dark blue with "Police," "County Police" or foreign lettering, plus battery-operated dome light. At least one foreign version exists: "Rijkspolitie," made for sale in the Netherlands.

465: Commer 15 cwt Pickup Truck, 90 mm, the same chassis-cab unit in red or yellow, with a semi-enclosed rear section in yellow or red; through 1965.

1128: Priestman Cub Shovel, 165 mm, with swiveling cab and working shovel, in yellow, orange and gray, on black rubber treads; through 1976.

1131: Bedford Carrimore Machinery Carrier, 241 mm, with a new blue Bedford cab pulling a silver-gray semi-trailer revised from that of 1104, now with two spare wheels in place of the earlier winch; through 1966.

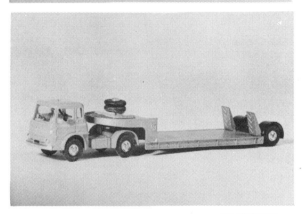

1133: US Army Troop Transporter, 140 mm, the olive 1118 International 6x6 with a few white decals; through 1965.

GS 21: ERF Milk Truck (456) and Trailer (101) with Milk Churns (1487); through 1966.

GS 24: Commer Construction Set, consisted of two of the new 15 cwt chassis-cab units and four rear bodies; milk truck, pickup, van and bus; through 1968.

153A: Bluebird, with aluminum wheels and other minor changes; through 1965.

1132: Carrimore Low Loader, 241 mm, a similar revision of 1100 in yellow and red, this being the low-side semi-trailer, likewise with spare wheels in place of the winch; through 1965.

GS 17: Land Rover (438) pulling the 154 Ferrari on a yellow trailer—as if Formula I Ferraris were ever seen in such low-budget operations! Through 1967.

GS 22: Farm Set, composed of 51, 57, 60, 61 (these two issued individually the next year), 1111, 1487 and 1490; through 1966.

GS 23: Circus Set, of 101, 406, 426 (later replaced by 503), 607, 1121 and two of 1123; through 1966.

GS 25: Shell Gas Station with five cars, three garages and all sorts of accessories; later a similar B. P. Gas Station; through 1966.

GS 27: Priestman Cub Shovel and Transporter (1128 and 1131); through 1972.

GS 28: Car Transporter (1105) with 222, 230, 232 and 234 as its load; shown in the 1963 and 1966 catalogs, presumably available in '64 and '65 as well.

1964: OLDTIMERS, PULLMAN AND DRIVING SCHOOL

The year of 1964 brought Corgi's first oldtime cars, an excellently modeled 1927 Bentley and 1915 Model T Ford, plus an interesting modern-day Mercedes 600 with working windshield wipers, a Buick with Trans-o-lite head- and taillights, and a pair of Driving School cars that steered via their roof signs. A wide variety of other models accompanied them:

60: Fordson Power Major Tractor, 83 mm, in blue, replacing the earlier 55 and including a driver among its improvements; through 1966.

155: Lotus-Climax 25 Formula I, 90 mm, in what was then correct Team Lotus green and yellow, with driver, windshield, steering wheel, mirrors, roll bar, engine block and exhausts. It was an excellent model, and I was sad to see it replaced in 1969 by a gaudy orange and white version with an aerofoil, 158.

236: Austin Cambridge A60 Motor School Car, 95 mm, in light or medium blue, complete with student and instructor, plus a large cylindrical roof sign which, when turned, steers the front wheels. Shown is the right-hand drive version; made through 1965.
255: Austin A60 Motor School Car, 95 mm, the left-hand drive version, in blue; through 1966.

245: 1964 Buick Riviera, 108 mm, in light blue, metallic blue or gold, with spoked wheels, plated grille and bumpers, and Trans-o-lite front and rear lights; through 1968.

247: Mercedes-Benz 600 Pullman, 121 mm, in metallic maroon, with not only working windshield wipers that can be turned on and off (the mechanism that makes them work can be viewed through the chassis panel), but also rear side windows that can be raised and lowered, plus the usual refinements of interior detail, chrome plating and such; an outstanding model, made through 1969 and prized today.

253: Mercedes-Benz 220SE Coupe, 121 mm, a metallic maroon revision of 230, complete with opening trunk, spare wheel and luggage as before, but without self-centering steering; through 1968.

302: Hillman Hunter, a rally car for the London-to-Sidney race; through 1970.

312: Jaguar E-Type, 95 mm, in chrome or gold finish with racing number, an open version of 307 but too flashy to come near equaling the hardtop's beauty; through 1968.

315: Simca 1000 Coupe, 90 mm, usually in chrome finish with racing stripes and number, but also in blue; through 1966.

317: Monte Carlo Mini-Cooper, 73 mm, a red and white version of 227, representing Paddy Hopkirk's 1964 Monte Carlo Rally winner, with racing number "37," rally decal and swiveling roof spotlight; through 1965, and followed by many other competition Minis.

354: Commer Army Ambulance, 90 mm, the previous year's 15 cwt van in olive with red cross decals, blue dome light and white lettering; through 1966.

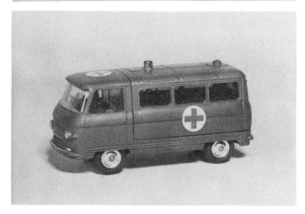

355: Commer Military Police Van, 90 mm, another variation on the theme, likewise in olive, with blue dome light, white star and lettering, and barred opaque rear windows; through 1965.

356: US Army Personnel Carrier, 91 mm, the 434 VW Kombi in olive, with white star and lettering; through 1966.

357: Land Rover Weapons Carrier, 95 mm, 438 in olive with white star decals and antenna—American forces in other countries may well use vehicles made there, but in this case it seems Corgi simply used whatever models were handy; through 1966.

358: 1961 Oldsmobile Super 88 US Army Staff Car, 108 mm, in olive with the usual decals, driver and three passengers; through 1966.

359: Karrier Army Field Kitchen, 91 mm, last seen as the Mister Softee truck, in olive with decals as usual, plus the swiveling vendor; through 1966.

447: Wall's Ice Cream Van, 90 mm, a Ford Thames pickup in blue with a striped house on the back, sliding windows, and separate figures of vendor and young customer; made through 1967 but accompanied from 1965 on by 474, the same truck with musical chimes played by a huge crank on the back of the truck.

448: Austin Police Mini-Van, 79 mm, commercial counterpart to the Mini, in dark blue with opening rear doors, "Police" lettering in white, antenna and figures of policeman and tracker dog; through 1969. In these two models we see the beginning of Corgi's inclination to offer separate plastic figures with some of their models.

450: Austin Mini-Van, 79 mm, a civilian version in light green, likewise with opening rear doors; through 1967.

463: Commer Ambulance, 90 mm, the 15 cwt chassis with bus body, painted white or cream, with dome light and rear windows in blue and "Ambulance" lettering in red; through 1966.

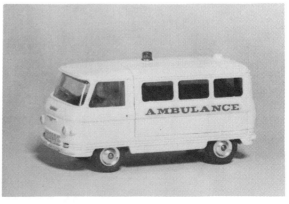

466: Commer Milk Float, 90 mm, a white 15 cwt chassis-cab with a load of milk bottles in cases, the rear covered by a light blue roof with pillars and lower skirt; through 1965.

468: Leyland London Transport Routemaster Bus, 114 mm, the typical red doubledecker, and a natural for Corgi, usually with "Corgi Toys" (first regular issue) or "Outspan" (second regular issue) side decals, but also used for several promotional issues: Gamages, Church's Shoes, Madame Tussaud's and Design Centre, all in red, plus light green, cream and brown Australian versions of the two regular types; in production through 1975, when the larger but otherwise similar 469 replaced it. One of Corgi's all-time favorites.

472: Land Rover Public Address Vehicle, 91 mm, in green with yellow open back and two loudspeakers, plus rotating candidate, woman precariously handing out pamphlets from the tailboard, and "Vote for Corgi" decals; through 1966, though it joined the circus a year before that as 487.

475: Citroen ID19 Safari Ski Club Car, 108 mm, in white with ski rack on the roof, separate skier and, at first, "Olympic Winter Sports" decals, just in time for the 1964 Olympics; later with "Corgi Ski Club" decals; through 1968, when a new version, 499, replaced it.

503: Giraffe Transporter, 97 mm, a Bedford chassis-cab in red with high blue box, the rear panel of which lowers to let the two plastic giraffes out; the model was produced through 1971.

9001: Bentley 1927 Tourer, 102 mm, a fine model in dark green with brown interior and black raised top, racing number and driver in white coveralls and helmet, plus other details including tool kit, huge horn and Union Jack decal; produced through 1969, and used in several other versions as well as this.

9011: Model T Ford, 83 mm, a 1915 tourer in the traditional black, excellently detailed with elderly driver and lady passenger attired for the occasion, spare wheel, folded top and superb suspension detail; through 1969.

1127: Bedford Simon Snorkel Fire Engine, 252 mm, in red with silver rear deck, yellow basket (holding one black fireman) at the end of its long arm, and unpainted retractable supporting jacks; through 1976, after which a new version (1126) replaced it.

61: Four Furrow Plough, 90 mm, in blue and silver, replacing 56; through 1970.

500: US Army Land Rover, 95 mm, apparently a rare variation of 357 issued only in 1964 and never shown in the catalog. It may never have reached the USA.

9013: Model T Ford, 83 mm, a top-up version in light blue with black top and interior, tan spoked wheels (9011's are black), and driver attempting to start the motor by cranking it—and looking as if he's slipped a disc. Produced, like the others, through 1969, when a factory fire destroyed the oldtimer dies.

GS 13: Fordson Tractor and Plough (60 and 61); through 1967.

GS 29: Massey-Ferguson Tractor and Trailer (50 and 51), replacing the older number 7; through 1965.

GS 31: Buick Riviera (245), pulling a boat and trailer that became 104 the next year; through 1968.

1965: GIMMICKS GALORE

Corgi's new issues for 1965 were not only more numerous than usual, but included a number of interesting models that would have been sufficient to make the year a memorable one even if the firm's most spectacular model had not been produced then. But it was, and it took the toy industry by storm. It was, of course, the first of Corgi's three James Bond Aston Martins. Not only did it include a wealth of special features, but it, along with the Saint's Volvo, forged the first links between Corgi Toys and the world of movies, television and comic strips—a connection that has grown closer ever since. The 1965 new issues were:

58: Beast Carrier Trailer, 112 mm, a yellow two-wheel trailer with red chassis and green webbing on top, carrying four plastic calves; through 1971.

62: Farm Tipper Trailer, 114 mm, structurally like the lower part of 58, with red tipper, yellow chassis, hydraulic cylinder and plastic raves (racks at each end) to hold the hay aboard; through 1971.

64: Forward Control Jeep FC-150 with Conveyor, 197 mm, the 409 pickup equipped with a two-section conveyor belt, its yellow framework attached to a white base mounted in the rear of the red truck; a crank moves the belts, and the two sections can tilt up or down. This different and ingenious model was produced through 1969.

104: Dolphin Cabin Cruiser on Trailer, 136 mm, the blue, white and red boat of the previous year's GS 31 on its red trailer; through 1968.

246: 1965 Chrysler Imperial Crown Convertible, 108 mm, in dark red or dark bluish-green with light blue interior, opening hood, trunk and doors (the first Corgi model to have all four), folding seats, two people and a set of golf clubs, and running on spoked diecast wheels; through 1968.

248: 1959 Chevrolet Impala, 108 mm, an update of 220 with suspension, in tan with a white roof and plenty of chrome; through 1967.

249: Morris Mini-Cooper Deluxe, 73 mm, the usual Mini casting in black with a red roof, featuring yellowish decals on its back and sides to simulate wickerwork; through 1968.

258: The Saint's Volvo P-1800, 90 mm, 228 in white with red interior, jeweled headlights and a decal with the Saint's haloed stick-drawing on the hood. While I can imagine Simon Templar (who is at the wheel) trading in his Hirondel for a Volvo, I simply cannot picture him flaunting his symbol on the hood! This version lasted through 1969; a new version, 201, replaced it the following year.

261: James Bond's Aston Martin DB5, 97 mm, in gold, with a bullet shield that pops up at the rear when one pushes the exhaust pipe, projecting rams and guns at the front that come out when one moves a lever on the left side of the car, and another lever farther back to rid Bond, who is at the wheel, of his sinister gun-toting passenger by opening a panel in the roof and ejecting him. It was in production through 1968, when a slightly larger and even more lethal version, 270, replaced it.

314: Ferrari Berlinetta 250 LeMans, 95 mm, in Ferrari red with racing number and emblem, with its rear body hinged to lift up, exposing the detailed engine compartment; a fine model, issued through 1971.

318: Lotus Elan S2, 90 mm, an open sports car in light blue, white or (in a gift set) green and yellow; (rally version with stripe); issued through 1968 and joined in 1967 by the 319 hard-top.

320: 1965 Ford Mustang Fastback Coupe, 95 mm, a very popular model in light green, dark blue, silver gray or lilac; its details included opening doors and spoked wire wheels; issued through 1967 in this form and used otherwise as well.

322: Monte Carlo Rover 2000, 95 mm, the 252 casting in maroon and white, with "136" and rally decals; through 1967.

323: Monte Carlo Citroen DS19, 210 in light blue and white, with the usual rally decals including number; through 1966.

470: Forward Control Jeep, 91 mm, a plastic-covered version of the 409 FC-150, in grayish blue or mustard with gray top; through 1972.

471: Mobile Canteen, 95 mm, a new Karrier in blue with "Joe's Diner" decals, a white plastic side panel lowering to form a counter, and Joe inside to dish out the food; through 1966.

478: Forward Control Jeep Tower Wagon, 129 mm, the open FC-150 as offered in GS 14, in green with unpainted arms holding a yellow overhead platform on which a workman stands, his arms upraised as though worshipping the sun; through 1969.

480: 1959 Impala Taxi, 108 mm, the new Chevrolet (248) in yellow and red, with taxi sign and decals, replacing 221; through 1969.

481: 1959 Chevrolet Impala Police Car, 108 mm, the same car in black and white, with dome light, "Police" hood decal and "Police Patrol" shield labels on the doors, replacing 223; through 1969.

482: 1959 Chevrolet Impala Fire Chief, 108 mm, the same car again in red and white, with dome light, "Fire Chief" hood decal and emblem labels on the doors, replacing 439; through 1969.

485: BMC Austin Mini-Countryman Estate Car, 79 mm, the Mini as station wagon, turquoise with tan 'wood,' roof rack, surfboards and even a male surfer, plus opening rear doors as on the Minivan; through 1969.

487: Land Rover Chipperfields Parade Vehicle, 91 mm, the "Vote for Corgi" 472 in circus red and blue, with rotating clown at the mike and a monkey too; through 1969.

9021: Daimler 1911 38-hp Open Tourer, 108 mm, a new oldtimer with orange-red body, yellow wheels and springs, chauffeur and little girl up front and her parents in back; a good model but somehow lacking the excellence of the Bentley and Ford; through 1969. By the way, the factory fire—or something—prevented the 9022 blue Daimler and the 9014 Ford Lyons Van from ever being issued.

9031: Renault 1910 12/16 Coupe, 102 mm, a closed car with lilac lower body, black chassis and top, wheels to match the body and nobody inside; through 1969.
9032: Renault 12/16 Coupe, the same car in yellow instead of lilac; through 1969, and comparable with the Bentley and Ford in quality.

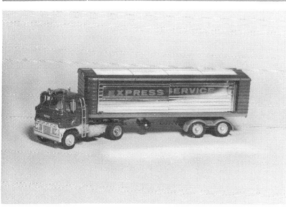

1137: Ford H-1000 Express Service, 273 mm, tiltcab semi-trailer truck; through 1969.

242: Fiat Jolly, 79 mm, replacing 240; the car is yellow and no longer equipped with the first type's canopy; through 1966.

321: Monte Carlo Mini-Cooper, 73 mm, in red and white like 317 but without that model's roof spotlight, with "52" and a sheet-metal sump guard; through 1967.

474: Musical Wall's Ice Cream Van, the earlier blue and cream 447 with a crank on the back to make the chimes play; through 1968.

477: Land Rover Breakdown Truck, 114 mm, successor to 417, with a redesigned yellow plastic cover, the usual red body, and a wrecker boom with working winch—plus suspension; it stayed in production through 1977—yes, 1977!

9002: Bentley 1927, 102 mm, this time in red with raised black top, civilian driver and no racing number; through 1969.

9012: Model T Ford, 86 mm, with yellow body, black chassis, interior and folded top, and the same old couple as before in the front seats; through 1969.

1134: Bedford US Army Tanker, 191 mm, the usual semi-trailer rig in olive with army decals; issued only in 1965.

1135: Army Heavy Equipment Transporter, 241 mm, the 1131 flat low loader in olive with army star decal; also made only in 1965.

GS 32; Massey-Ferguson Tractor with Shovel and Tipping Trailer (53 and 62); through 1967.

GS 33: Fordson Tractor and Beast Carrier (60 and 58); through 1967.

GS 35: Routemaster Bus, London Taxi (468 and 418) with policeman figure; through 1968.

GS 38: Monte Carlo Rally Set, with 321, 322 and 323; through 1967.

1966: BATMAN, THE MAN FROM U.N.C.L.E.–AND A RHINO

The funnies continued to make their mark on the relatively few new Corgis of 1966 with the Batmobile and the Man From U.N.C.L.E. Car. Neither could compare with James Bond's Aston. The oldtime series acquired its last member in the form of a 1912 Rolls-Royce, and on the sporting side a competition version of the Mustang was joined by the RAC Rally Mini, Monte Carlo Hillman and East African Safari Volkswagen, the last accompanied by a charging rhinoceros. The 1966 Corgis were:

66: Massey-Ferguson 165 Tractor, 76 mm, a new version of old 50, in red, white and gray; through 1973. 56: Four Furrow Plough.

67: Ford 5000 Tractor, 90 mm, a brand new model in blue and gray, with driver and various bits of chromed plastic or unpainted metal. The overhanging front of its hood distinguishes it from the vertical-front 60; through 1973. 61: Four Furrow Plough.

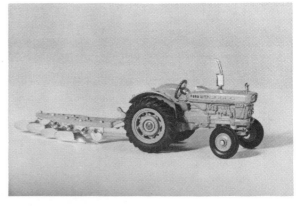

256: Volkswagen 1200 East African Safari Car, 91 mm, in dark orange plus number decals, Safari labels, opening front and rear hoods, and steering via the roof-mounted spare wheel—plus the aforementioned rhinoceros; through 1969.

259: Citroen DS19 'Le Dandy,' 102 mm, a jazzy sports coupe in either blue and white or metallic maroon, with jeweled headlights, opening doors and trunk, folding seat backs and spoked wheels; through 1969.

263: 1966 Rambler Marlin, 102 mm, a sleek fastback in red and black, with opening doors, folding seats, trailer hitch and spoked wheels; through 1969.

264: 1966 Oldsmobile Toronado, 108 mm, an interestingly atypical American car in peacock blue, with retractable headlights controlled by a small wheel under the fender, plus spoked wheels and a good deal of chrome; produced through 1969 and adapted in 1968 into 276.

267: Batmobile, 127 mm, black with a bit of red plus blue-tinted glass around the seats of Batman and Robin, equipped with chain-cutter blade in front, rocket-firing stacks amidship and plastic flames coming out the exhaust pipe as the wheels turn. Like the James Bond Aston, a big success; and still in production.

324: Marcos 1800GT, 91 mm, a sport coupe in white with green stripes or blue with white; its doors open, as does its entire hood, disclosing the engine with details in silver; wire wheels too; made in this form through 1969, then as 377.

325: Ford Mustang Competition Car, 95 mm, 320 in racing trim, painted white or silver with red stripes, wire wheels and opening doors; through 1969.

328: Monte Carlo Hillman Imp, 83 mm, 251 in its usual blue plus Monte Carlo Rally decals and "107;" replaced by a very similar 340 in 1977.

440: Ford Cortina Estate Car, 95 mm, in blue with simulated wood trim, jeweled headlights, opening tailgate and figures of golfer, caddy and golf bag; through 1967, when it was revised as 491.

492: Volkswagen Police Car, 91 mm, the Safari car in police colors for Germany (Polizei; green and white), the Netherlands (Politie) and Switzerland (both white), and possibly others, each with appropriate decals, the usual opening hoods, and steering via the blue dome light and its mounting; through 1969, replaced in 1970 by 373.

497: The Man From U.N.C.L.E. Car, 108 mm, the old 1961 Oldsmobile Super 88 in dark blue or cream, with a sort of spotlight on the roof that, when pushed, makes a popping noise and moves the two characters in and out as if they're shooting; a big label on the hood; through 1969.

9041: Rolls-Royce 1912 Silver Ghost, 118 mm, a handsome silver oldtimer with black chassis and brown interior; its withdrawal late in 1970, the last victim of the factory fire, brought the oldtimer series to an untimely and ill-deserved end and made rarities of them. It was also used in 1970 as the 805 Hardy Boys' Car.

1138: Ford H-1000 Auto Transporter, 273 mm, with orange Ford tiltcab and blue and silver Carrimore Mark IV semi-trailer, capable of carrying six cars; through 1969.

333: RAC Rally Mini-Cooper, 73 mm, red and white as usual, with "21" and RAC decals plus sump guard; issued only in 1966.

1140: Mobilgas Tanker, 191 mm, the newer type Bedford cab and the usual tank semi-trailer, in red as before with blue and white Mobilgas logo; through 1967.

1141: Milk Tanker, 191 mm, the same cab and trailer in blue and white; through 1967. I wonder why Corgi only got around to putting the second Bedford cab on the two tankers when they were removing it from the car carrier. . . .

GS 46: All Winners, including 264 or 310, 312, 314, 324 and 325; through 1969.

GS 47: Ford Tractor (67) with a conveyor trailer made by mounting the conveyor unit from the Jeep pickup on a four-wheel trailer; through 1969.

GS 48: Ford Auto Transporter (1138) and six cars; through 1969.

1967: AVENGERS TO ZAGATO

In 1967, as in 1966, relatively few new models were issued, but they included the Avengers gift set, a Lincoln Continental, a new Corvette, a highly detailed Holmes Wrecker and other noteworthy models. A change to a slightly larger scale, about 1/43, also began. The new models were:

69: Massey-Ferguson 165 Tractor with Shovel, 127 mm, the red and gray, 66 with an unpainted working shovel; through 1973.

71: Tandem Disc Harrow, 90 mm, in yellow and red, with adjustable banks of harrow blades; through 1971.

156: 1966 Cooper-Maserati Formula I, 90 mm, a good companion for the 155 Lotus, in Rob Walker's dark blue with white nose band and red number 7, complete with driver, detailed engine and exhaust pipes; changed in 1969 to the yellow and white 159.

262: 1967 Lincoln Continental Limousine, 149 mm, in gold with black roof, later blue and tan, with opening doors, hood and trunk, jeweled headlights, and a battery to light up a color television screen inside—another Corgi first. Produced through 1969, and very desirable today.

319: Lotus Elan SL Hardtop, 90 mm, companion to the open 318, in blue and white, red and white or (in a set) yellow and green; through 1968.

327: MGB GT, 90 mm, the first of three MGB and MGC Corgis, in red, with opening doors and trunk and folding seats; through 1968, when it was replaced by 345.

330: Porsche Carrera 6, 97 mm, in blue and white or red and white, with name, emblem and number decals, racing wheels, and a raising rear body with engine beneath it; through 1969, replaced the next year by the whizz-wheeled 371 version.

332: Lancia Fulvia Zagato, 91 mm, a metallic blue fastback with opening doors, folding seats and patterned wheels; through 1969, replaced by 372 in 1970.

337: 1963 Chevrolet Corvette Sting Ray Stock Car, 95 mm, a silly sort of car in yellow with too many decals and too much chrome, including air intakes coming through a gap in the hood and heavy exhaust pipes with mufflers below the doors; through 1969, with the same casting used in 1970 for the slightly more sane 376.

339: Monte Carlo Mini-Cooper, 73 mm, yet another red and white rally car (left) with "177," the usual decals, and even a rally label on its sump guard, plus a chromed plastic roof rack with two spare wheels; through 1972. 308: Monte Carlo Mini-Cooper (right).

340: Monte Carlo Sunbeam Imp, 83 mm, a rehash of 328, no longer called a Hillman but still painted blue, with "77" and other decals; through 1968.

483: Dodge D600 Kew Fargo Dump Truck, 136 mm, with white cab, black chassis and blue operating tipper; through 1972.

484: Dodge D600 Kew Fargo Farm Stake Truck, 140 mm, the same cab in tan with a green stake body and, believe it or not, five pigs; through 1971. These two trucks represent the British Dodge truck with a six-cylinder Perkins Diesel engine.

486: 1959 Chevrolet Kennel Service Wagon, 108 mm, a light van in red and white, with "Kennel Club" labels, a picture of a dachshund above the cab that seems to run as one changes one's angle of vision, sliding side panels, opening tailgate and a cargo of dogs; through 1969, used as 511 in 1970.

490: Volkswagen Breakdown Van, 102 mm, an open tan or white pickup with its rear bed full of equipment and an operating winch; through 1971.

494: Bedford Earth Dumper, 102 mm, a modern Bedford cab with quarry dumper like that of the 458 ERF, in red and yellow, blue and yellow, or yellow and blue; through 1972.

1142: Holmes Ford H1000 Wrecker, 114 mm, a mighty machine in red, white and black, complete with tiltcab, horns, ladders, spare wheels, warning light and all that, plus two golden wrecker booms that can work independently or together; a fine model produced through 1974 and revised the next year, with the Ford tiltcab replaced by a Berliet.

491: Ford Cortina Estate Car, 95 mm, a revised 440 in either gray or red with simulated wood, retaining the golfer, caddy and golf bag; through 1969.

9004: World of Wooster 1927 Bentley, 102 mm, good old 9001 without its raised top, in red or green, with Jeeves at the wheel and an insouciant Bertie Wooster, monocle and all, leaning casually in the direction of the radiator shell; through 1969.

GS 36: Rambler Marlin (263) and Speedboat on Trailer, issued thus through 1968 and for two more years with the same number, but with the Rambler replaced by the Olds Toronado.

GS 37: Lotus Racing Team, with the 155 Formula I car, green and yellow 318, yellow and green 319, 490 VW Wrecker and the trailer formerly used for the Ferrari in GS 17; through 1969.

GS 40: The Avengers, based on a television thriller, with John Steed in a green 1927 Bentley and Emma Peel beside a white Lotus Elan convertible; through 1969.

GS 45: A second All Winners set of sports cars (261, 310, 314, 324 and 325), was never issued, nor was the 9014 Model T Ford Lyons Tea Van, both in the 1967 catalog.

1968: CHITTY CHITTY GOLDEN JACKS

Golden Jacks were Corgi's most notable innovation for 1968. They consisted of four small levers, one inboard of each wheel, which in their closed position held the wheels on the axles; when opened, they allowed removal of the wheels and provided support for the car when one or more wheels were off. They must have led to thousands of lost wheels and parental complaints! They were not one of Corgi's more successful new ideas, and disappeared from the scene in 1970. But the use of movie and comic-strip characters' cars continued: James Bond had two cars to choose from, Batman had a boat, the Green Hornet had his Black Beauty, and Chitty Chitty Bang Bang was here—and as if that weren't enough, the Mustang appeared with psychedelic labels. The new Corgis for 1968 were:

107: Batboat on Trailer, 140 mm, a black and red plastic boat on a gold diecast trailer; still in production, its wheels and tires replaced by Whizzwheels.

109: Pennyburn Workmen's Trailer, 76 mm, a blue box with hinged lid on a yellow chassis, containing a red load of tools; through 1969.

266: Chitty Chitty Bang Bang, 162 mm, a pseudo-vintage open tourer with silver hood, coppery brown rear body and black chassis, plus such extras as huge jeweled headlights, red jeweled taillights, and a bulb horn that looks like somebody's pet alligator—plus red and orange striped wings. A family of four is aboard. The name, of course, was taken from Count Louis Zborowski's Brooklands racing cars of the early twenties, which had only one 'Chitty' and bears no resemblance to this model; produced through 1972.

268: The Green Hornet's Black Beauty, 127 mm, a black beast of 1965 Ford Galaxie parentage and overtones of Lincoln Continental, with Green Hornet roof decal, the man (or insect?) shooting from the right rear window, the trunk opening to disgorge a weapon rather like a large red plastic steering wheel, and the radiator grille falling away to expose a weapon resembling a trench mortar. The last two features are operated by large levers on the left side of the car; through 1972.

270: James Bond's Aston Martin DB5, 102 mm, a slightly larger version, in silver gray, of the original issue, with all its refinements plus triangular red plastic rear hubcaps to slash at anything that comes too close; replaced in 1965 by a third type, 271, but kept in production through 1977.

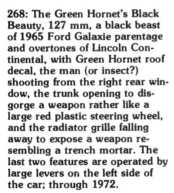

275: Rover 2000TC, 95 mm, in dark green, maroon or gold, with amber tinted windows, a black plastic spare wheel case on the trunk lid and . . . Golden Jacks! Produced through 1970, replaced the next year by 281, minus the last two innovations.

334: Mini-Magnifique, 73 mm, in metallic green or blue with opening hood, doors and trunk, chromed engine block, bumpers and trim, and a red-and-yellow striped roof hatch covered by clear plastic; through 1970.

335: Jaguar E-Type 2 + 2, 108 mm, noticeably larger than such contemporaries as the Torona-do, to say nothing of the earlier E-Type, in maroon or blue, with opening hood, rear hatch and doors, chromed engine and bumpers, wire wheels and cop-per-colored exhaust pipes; a fine model despite its size, it was withdrawn at the end of 1969 and replaced by the updated 374 in 1970.

336: James Bond's Toyota 2000, 102 mm, a sleek white sports roadster with an Oriental lady (I think) driving and The Man shooting, a red antenna with pennant, and a lever that opens a trunk full of rockets. Produced through 1969, then issued as a somewhat less potent but pleas-ant sports car, 375.

338: 1968 Chevrolet Camaro SS350, 102 mm, a sporting hardtop in lime gold with black plastic top, red interior, opening doors and Golden Jacks; produced through 1970, revised the next year as 304, without Golden Jacks.

341: Mini-Marcos 850GT, 86 mm, a little maroon fastback with opening hood, clear plastic headlight shields, wire wheels, name decals and Golden Jacks; produced through 1970 and revived in 1972 as 305.

345: MGC GT Competition Car, 90 mm, in yellow with black hood and trunk lid, the latter opening, as do the doors, plus jeweled headlights and wire wheels; a handsome little car, differing from the 327 MGB only in the power bulge on its hood; issued through 1969, then revised as 378.

479: Commer Mobile Camera Van, 90 mm, a dark blue and white minibus with a platform holding a TV camera and its operator; through 1971; the casting also used for 508.

499: 1968 Citroen ID19 Olympic Winter Sports, 108 mm, an updated 475 in white with blue roof, Grenoble (site of the 1968 Winter Olympics) decal on the hood, a roof rack of skiing equipment and a man on a diecast gold sled; through 1969.

506: Police 'Panda' Sunbeam Imp, 83 mm, a version of 340 in white and black or light blue and white, with police decals and blue dome light; through 1971.

508: Commer Holiday Camp Special Minibus, 90 mm, the same casting as the TV Camera Van, in orange and white with bright decals and a load of luggage on its roof rack; through 1969.

1143: American LaFrance Ladder Truck, 285 mm, a magnificent model in red with white decks and yellow ladders, gold equipment and black-coated firemen; still produced.

276: Oldsmobile Toronado, 108 mm, in maroon or gold, an updated 264 with Golden Jacks; through 1970.

348: Psychedelic Mustang, 95 mm, 320 in light blue with red-orange-yellow decals in the style of the times; apparently issued only in 1968.

498: Mini-Countryman, 79 mm, meant to be 485 without the surfboards but was never issued.

GS 1: Ford Tractor and Beast Carrier (67 and 58); through 1972.

GS 3: Batmobile, Batboat and Trailer (267 and 107); still in production.

GS 5: Agricultural Set, with 62, 69, 71, 438 and 484; through 1972.

GS 6: VW Racing Tender (a version of 490) and Cooper-Maserati (156) on trailer; through 1969.

GS 7: Daktari Set, based on the television program, with camouflage-striped Land Rover and figures; through 1975.

GS 9: Massey-Ferguson Tractor with Shovel and Tipping Trailer (69 and 62); through 1973.

GS 10: Rambler Marlin (263), Camping Trailer (a version of 109), and roof rack with kayaks; through 1969.

GS 12: Grand Prix Racing Set, with Formula I Lotus and Cooper (155 and 156), Porsche Carrera 6 (330), VW Racing Tender as in GS 6, and trailer; through 1972.

1969: BEATLES AND MONKEES

It was only a matter of time until Corgi met the world of rock music, and it happened in 1969 with the appearance of the Monkeemobile and the Beatles' Yellow Submarine. It was also the year of Pop Art, and of controversy over aerofoils on Grand Prix cars, both of which had their effect on the year's new issues:

74: Ford 5000 Tractor with Scoop, 90 mm, 67 in its usual blue with something like a back hoe mounted on its side; through 1972.

158: Lotus-Climax Formula I, 90 mm, 155 in orange and white with a chromed plastic aerofoil; through 1971.

159: Cooper-Maserati Formula I, 90 mm, 156 in yellow and white, also with a chrome wing; through 1971.

271: DeTomaso Ghia Mangusta, 97 mm, in light blue and white with body and chassis that detach from one another. Like the Renault's seat adjusters, this new idea was used only once. Replaced in 1970 by 203.

277: Monkeemobile, 127 mm, a long red top-up tourer with white roof, yellow interior, figures of the four Monkees, chromed engine set in a well in the hood, two chromed nostril-type radiator grilles, and "Monkees" decals shaped like guitars; through 1970.

342: Lamborghini Miura P400, 95 mm, in yellow or red, with opening front and rear hoods, a small, opening trunk lid as well, black hood vents and rear window slats, and a plastic fighting bull (Lamborghini's trademark); intended to be produced with Golden Jacks but actually made with Whizzwheels, one of the first models to have them—unless it originally had the type of wheels used on the 343 Pontiac; through 1972, reappearing in 1974 as 319.

343: 1968 Pontiac Firebird Convertible, 102 mm, a silver open car with black trim, red interior, folding seats, opening doors and chromed air scoops; announced with Golden Jacks, it was issued first with rubberized plastic tires, metal wheels and red plastic central hubs, and later with Whizzwheels; through 1972.

344: Ferrari Dino 206, 104 mm, a mid-engined racing machine in yellow with black doors or red with white, black front and rear aerofoils and interior, racing number decals, and blue-tinted engine compartment cover; like the Pontiac, it was announced with Golden Jacks but appeared first with three-piece fast wheels and later with Whizzwheels; through 1973.

347: Chevrolet Astro I, 102 mm, a metallic blue 'car of the future' with lifting rear body that hoists two seats and their occupants up with it, a gold triangle on the hood, and three-piece wheels that gave way to Whizzwheels; through 1974.

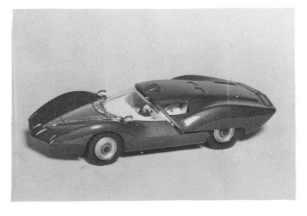

801: Noddy's Car, 95 mm, a wide, short yellow and red roadster holding three cartoon characters; through 1975, later revised as 804 with Noddy alone.

803: The Beatles' Yellow Submarine, 133 mm, yellow and white with multicolored trim but only vaguely resembling a submarine (or anything else), with opening hatches and figures of the four Beatles, plus four revolving periscopes; through 1970.

1139: Scammell Ford Circus Menagerie Transporter, 232 mm, a flatbed semi-trailer in the usual Chipperfields colors, carrying three occupied animal cages; through 1972.

1144: Circus Crane Truck and Cage, 200 mm, a stubby red and blue crane truck with the same cab as 1139—and one of the cages from it as well; through 1972.

GS 13: Tour de France Film Unit, with white and black Renault 16 borrowing the TV camera and operator of 479, plus a rounded roof sign, "Tour de France" decals and a racing cyclist; through 1972.

260: Renault 16TS, 91 mm, in metallic maroon, with opening hood, spare wheel, and seat backs that adjust via controls on the bottom of the car; replaced in 1970 by 202.

269: DAF City Car, 73 mm, never issued as such but revised as 283 in 1970.

349: Pop-Art Mini-Mostest, 73 mm, an orange-red Mini with decals even sillier than those on the Psychedelic Mustang; apparently issued only in 1969.

507: Chrysler Imperial Bermuda Taxi, 108 mm, meant to be the successor to the good old T-bird, but never issued.

650 and 651: BOAC and Air France Concorde Airliners, 190 mm; through 1972 and 1971 respectively, but reissued later.

1111: Massey-Ferguson Combine Harvester, 172 mm, an updated model, still in red with yellow parts, but those parts are now made of plastic; through 1973.

1148: Scammell Carrimore Car Transporter, 273 mm, the same cab unit, this time in red and white, with a six-car semi-trailer much like that of 1138 in the same red and white; issued only in 1969, replaced in 1970 by a new three-decker, 1146.

GS 8: Lions of Longleat, with striped Land Rover, three lions and their den, and three joints of meat, fortunately made of plastic! Through 1974.

GS 14: Giant Daktari Set, with the green-and-black Land Rover of GS 7, versions of the 484 Farm Truck and 503 Giraffe Truck, and all sorts of wild life; through 1973.

GS 15: Land Rover and Horse Box Trailer, 438 plus a new trailer issued the following year as 112; through 1977.

GS 21: Circus Crane Truck and Menagerie Truck (1144 and 1139); through 1971.

GS 25: VW Racing Tender and Cooper Formula I, a new version of the previous year's GS 6 with the new 159 Cooper; through 1971.

GS 36: Oldsmobile Toronado (276) and Speedboat on Trailer, the Toronado replacing the Rambler used in this set in 1967 and '68; through 1970.

1970: FAST CARS AND WHIZZWHEELS

The many models deleted at the end of 1969 were more than compensated for by the numerous new releases of 1970. The new models included everything from Popeye's Paddle Wagon and the Hardy Boys' Rolls-Royce to a Lunar Bug and a farm tractor with a buzzsaw. But the big news was Whizzwheels; one-piece plastic castings that united tires, wheels and hubcaps and, appropriately, moved fast, for many of the new models or revisions that were equipped with them were models of fast cars. New for 1970 were:

72: Ford 5000 Tractor with Trencher, 138 mm, the usual blue tractor with a scoop like that of 74 moved to the rear; through 1974.

73: Massey-Ferguson 165 Tractor with Saw, 90 mm, the usual 66 in red and gray with a yellow attachment holding a circular saw, plus a shield for the driver and "realistic engine noise;" through 1973.

112: Rice's Beaufort Double Horse Box, 102 mm, the blue and white trailer from GS 15, with mare, foal and gates that become ramps; through 1971.

201: The Saint's Volvo P-1800, 90 mm, an updated 258, still in white, but with a red and white hood label and Whizzwheels; through 1972.

**202: Renault 16TS, 91 mm, a
revised 260 in dark metallic
blue, with Whizzwheels but without the adjustable seats of the
earlier type; through 1972.**

**203: DeTomaso Mangusta, 97
mm, a revision of 271 in dark
green with gold stripes and
Whizzwheels, without a detachable chassis; through 1973.**

**273: Rolls-Royce Silver Shadow,
120 mm, in gray and white, with
Golden Jacks, issued for a short
time, then replaced later in the
year by 280.**

**274: Bentley T Series, 120 mm,
in rose red with black trim,
opening doors, hood and trunk,
with dashboard detail label, folding seat backs, and engine details in black and chrome, running on Whizzwheels; through
1973.**

282: Rally BMC Mini-Cooper, 73 mm, the Mini again, this time in white with black hood and doors, black and orange roof stripes and racing number 177; through 1974.

283: DAF City Car, 73 mm, successor to the stillborn 269, a stubby minicar in dark orange with black textured roof, opening hood, rear hatch and right-side doors, sliding left door, tilting seat backs and amber headlights; through 1974.

300: Corvette Sting Ray, 102 mm, a flashy but realistic model in shimmering maroon or green with black opening hood, retracting headlights, amber plastic transparent roof over the seats, Corvette emblems fore and aft, and Golden Jacks—the last Corgi to have them. The 1970 catalog called it "no longer in production," but it remained through 1972, side by side with 387.

301: Iso Grifo, 102 mm, a flat, sleek coupe in dark blue with black opening hood, engine details, a silver stripe across the roof, opening doors, adjustable seats and Whizzwheels; through 1973.

303: Roger Clark's Ford Capri, 102 mm, a white competition car with black hood, racing number 73, opening doors, and three-piece wheels later replaced by Whizzwheels; through 1972.

311: Ford Capri 3-Liter V6, 102 mm, the same casting in either red with black hood or electric dark orange threatening to become hot pink, with the same two types of wheels; through 1971, reissued as 331 in 1974.

313: Ford Cortina GXL, 102 mm, hinted at in the 1970 catalog as "Project X," and turned out to be a metallic bluish-green or copper hardtop with black textured roof, opening doors, adjusting seats, Whizzwheels and a jolly figure of Graham Hill; through 1973.

373: Volkswagen 1200 Police Car, 91 mm, successor to 492, in Anglo-American black and white, German white and green, and white for Holland and Belgium—and maybe more? Through 1976, with the same casting appearing in civilian form as 383.

374: Jaguar E-Type 2 + 2 V-12, 108 mm, the reissued 335 in red or yellow, with black plastic exhaust pipes—and, of course, Whizzwheels; through 1976.

375: Toyota 2000GT, 102 mm, in blue or purple, a revision of James Bond's 336, with Whizzwheels; through 1972.

376: Corvette Sting Ray Stock Car, 95 mm, a silver-gray version of the yellow 337, with black hood panel and racing numbers, but without the other decals; through 1972.

377: Marcos 3-Liter, 91 mm, the same body style as the 1800GT (324), in dark yellow or metallic green, the former with a black hood stripe plus Marcos emblem, the latter with only the emblem label, with new engine details and Whizzwheels; through 1973.

378: MGC GT, 90 mm, 345 revised, with reddish-orange body, black hood and Whizzwheels; through 1972.

380: Alfa Romeo P33 Pininfarina, 95 mm, a white open roadster with red and black interior, gold or black aerofoil, small black front wings and Whizzwheels; through 1974.

381: Volkswagen G. P. Beach Buggy, 69 mm, an interesting novelty in red or blue with black interior, white plastic top including a rack for two surfboards, engine details as part of the unpainted base, hood decal and Whizzwheels; through 1976.

382: Porsche 911S Targa, 95 mm, a typical Porsche coupe in metallic blue or green with black top, gold stripe, opening doors and engine hood, jeweled headlights and Whizzwheels; through 1975, also adapted for use as the 509 police car.

383: Volkswagen 1200, 91 mm, in civilian red with green base or orange with white, also appearing in Swiss P.T.T. yellow and German A.D.A.C. yellow and white; through 1976, later also used for a rally version numbered 384 after the life span of regular 384.

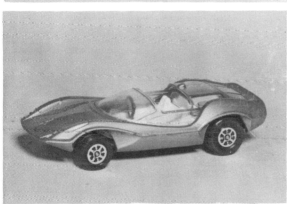

384: Adams Brothers Probe 16, 97 mm, futuristic but a little less unlikely than the Astro, in metallic maroon or gold, with blue-tinted dome over the white interior, one part of the dome sliding backward to serve as a door; through 1973.

385: Porsche 917, 108 mm, a racing machine in red or blue, with amber tinted windows, lifting rear hood and silver interior, plus racing number and name labels; through 1976.

386: Bertone Barchetta Runabout, 83 mm, a blend of beach buggy and idea car in yellow, with black interior and trim and an odd sort of wing; through 1973.

387: Chevrolet Corvette, 102 mm, 300 without Golden Jacks (and with Whizzwheels), in red or blue with black opening hood and other details as before; through 1973.

388: Mercedes-Benz C-111, 104 mm, the rotary-engined experimental car in orange with black lower body, opening gullwing doors, Star of Stuttgart label on the nose and the usual Whizzwheels; through 1974.

462: Commer Van, 90 mm, not in the catalog but used as one of three white and blue promotionals by the Co-Op supermarket chain in 1970 and a green-yellow-tan Hammonds promotional model in 1971; the usual 15 cwt casting, of course.

509: Porsche Targa Police Car, 95 mm, the 382 coupe in white with red doors and hoods, black roof, orange "Polizei" on white panels all around, a blue light on the left and a white loud-speaker, siren or perhaps radar gun on the trunk lid; through 1972.

510: Citroen DS21 Tour de France Team Manager's Car, 108 mm, a sort of streamlined pickup in red with "Paramount" decals on the sides, "Tour de France" and Tricolor on the hood, yellow interior and rear bed with a rack of spare wheels and the team manager with a megaphone; through 1972.

511: Performing Poodles Pickup, 108 mm, the 1959 Chevrolet Kennel Van (486) in light blue and red Chipperfields livery, new name labels but the same dachshund over the cab, plus a green ring, the poodles and their trainer; it runs, for a change, on the same cast wheels and black tires as its predecessor; through 1972.

513: Citroen ID19 Alpine Rescue Car, 108 mm, the usual Safari in white with red roof, equip-ment on it, "Alpine Rescue" labels, and figures of rescuer and St. Bernard dog; cast wheels and tires like the Poodles Pick-up; through 1972.

802: Popeye's Paddle Wagon, 127 mm, a fantastic creation that is now quite a rarity, with yellow body, red fenders, light blue paddlewheel covers, white deck, Olive Oyl rocking from side to side at the wheel, Popeye behind her peering to left and right through his telescope, the heads of Wimpy and Bluto bobbing up and down (all this motion caused by the turning of the wheels), and Swee' Pea rocking in a lifeboat at the stern; through 1972.

804: Noddy's Car, 95 mm, a revised 801 with Noddy alone; through 1977.

805: The Hardy Boys' 1912 Rolls-Royce, 118 mm, the 9041 oldtimer jazzed up in red, yellow and blue, with a green panel on the roof rack holding the figures of the Hardy Boys—one of whom is not a boy! Produced only in 1970.

806: Lunar Bug, 127 mm, a red-white-blue craft with four wheels on adjustable struts; its tailgate becomes a ramp, "just the thing for taking your Corgi Rockets and Corgi Juniors on a trip to the Moon!" says the catalog; through 1972.

1145: Mercedes-Benz Unimog with Dumper, 171 mm, the cab unit of 406 pulling a two-wheel gooseneck dumper in yellow plus red or blue; through 1976.

1147: Scammell Covered Semi-Trailer, 235 mm, with the same yellow and white cab and a yellow low-side semi-trailer with black "Ferrymasters" logo on its yellow plastic cover; through 1972.

1150: Mercedes-Benz Unimog Snow Plough, 155 mm, the 406 truck with an adjustable plough blade and red warning flags, in green and orange with olive top; through 1977.

1151: Mack Exxon Tanker, 278 mm, white with Exxon logo, never in the catalog but sold briefly about 1970. Oddly enough, one source gives 1151 as the number of the three-piece Co-Op set, composed of 462, 466 and 1147 in light blue and white, sold in Co-Op grocery stores during the 1970 Christmas season.

280: Rolls-Royce Silver Shadow, 120 mm, in blue and silver, later in solid dark blue, the revised 273 with Whizzwheels instead of Golden Jacks plus all the refinements of the Bentley; through 1978.

284: Citroen SM, 114 mm, a sleek, handsome car in modern Citroen style, with lime or lilac body, opening doors with chromed window frame/liner inserts, opening rear hatch and inner trunk cover, and cast wheels with plastic tires giving way to a newer type of spoked wheels; through 1975.

371: Porsche Carrera 6, 97 mm, a revised 330 in the same white and red, with Whizzwheels; through 1973.

372: Lancia Fulvia Zagato, 91 mm, 332 reissued in orange and black, with Whizzwheels; through 1972.

406: Mercedes-Benz Unimog, 91 mm, a stubby covered truck in yellow and blue, red and yellow or yellow and green, with olive or tan rear cover, black plastic rear-view mirrors on all but the yellow and green version, jeweled headlights (believe it or not), and red wheels with black heavy-tread tires; through 1976.

652 and 653: Japan Air Lines and Air Canada versions of the Concorde.

1146: Scammell Car Transporter, 290 mm, the yellow and white Handyman MK III cab from 1148 pulling a new three-tier six-car transporter; through 1973.

GS 20: Scammell Car Transporter (1147) with a full load of six cars; through 1973.

1971: IT'S A DRAGSTER

After all the Corgi activity of 1970, a period of calm could be expected to set in, as indeed it did for the next few years. The new issues of 1971 were not even half as numerous as those of 1970, and there were no remarkable new innovations to be seen. The most notable trend of the new Corgis was a leaning toward dragsters, with four of them going into production:

161: Commuter Dragster, 123 mm, long and skinny, metallic dark red with "Ford Commuter" and Union Jack decals, unpainted engine, plastic exhaust pipes, steering and suspension, and two types of spoked wheels; through 1973.

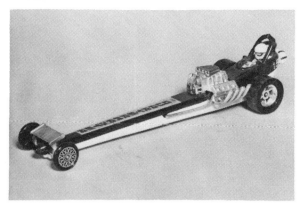

162: Quartermaster Dragster, 146 mm, green above, white below, with aerofoil above the front axle and engine just ahead of the driver, plus "Quartermaster" label; through 1972.

163: Glo-Worm Dragster, 113 mm, a white and blue Ford Capri with loads of labels on a body that lifts to expose a red chassis with black engine and white-suited driver; through 1976.

166: Mustang Organ Grinder Dragster, 102 mm, in yellow with green lettering, a green-tinted windshield that covers the engine compartment, too, red interior and bumpers, eight organ-pipe exhausts and a driver who looks like a Michelin advertisment; through 1974.

281: Rover 2000TC, 95 mm, in metallic grape with amber-tinted windows (including most of the roof) and Whizzwheels; a revision of 275; through 1973.

306: Morris Marina, 98 mm, a tasteful fastback coupe in maroon or lime gold, with opening doors and hood; through 1973.

312: Marcos Mantis, 110 mm, sleek and flat with metallic maroon body, opening doors, silver base, bumpers and grille, and spoked wheels of the second type used on the 284 Citroen; through 1973.

316: Ford GT-70, 92 mm, in light metallic green with black opening panel over the rear engine, name and number labels, and spoked wheels as on the Mantis; through 1973.

389: Reliant Bond Bug 700ES, 67 mm, a wedge-shaped three-wheeler in orange or light green, with the upper body lifting to give access to the interior, two big bugeye headlights, and name decals; produced through 1974, and *not* to be confused with the James Bond Moon Buggy!

391: James Bond's 1972 Ford Mustang Mach I, 113 mm, a typical American sporty coupe in red with black hood and white base, opening doors, chromed wheels and wide tires; no connection with James Bond is visible. Produced in this form through 1973, and revised then as 329.

1100: Mack Trans Continental Truck, 257 mm, in orange and blue-green, with long-nose cab and enclosed semi-trailer whose black side panels bear the "Trans Continental" logo; through 1973.

1106: Mack Container Truck, 290 mm, the same cab with a flat semi-trailer carrying two plastic containers, in yellow and red; perhaps not issued until 1972, produced through 1978.

1152: Mack Esso Tanker, 278 mm, the same cab again, white with black chassis, and a white tank semi with red chassis, Esso logo and "simulated delivery hoses;" through 1975.

304: Chevrolet Camaro SS 350, 102 mm, another revision, this time of 338, in blue or turquoise with white top, trim and base; through 1973.

467: Range Rover Police Car, 108 mm, in white with various trim depending on the nationality, as it exists in at least British and Netherlands versions; it may not have been put on the market until 1972; still in production.

807: Dougal's Magic Roundabout Car, 118 mm, a yellow Citroen pickup (same casting as 510) with *red* Whizzwheels, carrying three characters known as Dougal, Dylan and Brian Snail; through 1974.

1153: Priestman Cub Boom Crane, 230 mm, in red and yellow, running on black treads, swiveling on its base, with a yellow grab working from its silver boom by means of a winch atop the cab; through 1974.

GS 2: Unimog with Dumper and Priestman Shovel (1145 and 1128); through 1973.

GS 11: London Set, with Routemaster Bus, Austin Taxi and Mini (468, 418 and 226); through 1974—the last use of the 226 Mini.

GS 26: Beach Buggy (381) and sailboat on trailer (not issued separately); through 1976.

1972: A NEW GRAND PRIX SERIES

Even fewer new models were produced by Corgi in 1972 than in 1971, but they offered quite some variety. There were the first few members of a new 1/36 scale Formula I series, two more dragsters, James Bond's Moon Buggy, Mr. McHenry's Trike (pulling a box inhabited by one Zebedee, of uncertain species), and the gimmick of the year—Basil Brush's Car with canned laughter. The new models were:

164: Ford Anglia Wild Honey Dragster, 71 mm, a stubby yellow car with high prewar bodywork, green tinted windows and roof, engine where you'd expect the driver, driver in what ought to be the back seat, red "Wild Honey" and "Jaguar Powered" lettering and Whizzwheels; through 1973.

165: Adams Brothers Drag-Star, 113 mm, a four-engined monster in orange and red, with eight stub exhausts per engine, rear bumper (or something) that comes out when you push the pointed nosepiece, and enclosed driver; through 1974.

204: Morris Mini-Minor, 73 mm, a newer casting than 226, in orange or dark blue, with Whizzwheels; through 1973, also used as 308.

305: Mini-Marcos GT 850, 86 mm, a revised 341 ready to race, with red-white-blue stripes on its white body, racing number and Whizzwheels; through 1973.

393: Mercedes-Benz 350SL, 102 mm, in white or metallic dark blue with opening doors and hood (which includes the grille), running on at least two types of chromed spoked wheels; through 1979.

395: Fire Bug, 83 mm, the Beach Buggy in orange with no roof, but rather a chromed rack holding a pair of yellow ladders that also rest on the windshield; an entertaining but quite unreal novelty produced through 1973.

681: Stunt Motorcycle, 80 mm, a gold cycle with driver in blue coveralls and yellow helmet, the whole thing mounted on a red plastic base with four red wheels, not in the catalog but issued in 1962 or '63 to run down the Corgi Rockets track.

808: Basil Brush's Car, 95 mm, an antique 1911 Renault of sorts in red and yellow, with a huge plastic Basil filling the driver's seat and his tail (he's a fox, you see) emerging beside him—plus " 'laugh' tapes and sound box." I've never had the slightest desire to hear Basil laugh, so I can't tell you how he sounds. Made through 1973.

859: Mr. McHenry's Trike, 117 mm, a red tricycle with no visible source of power, not even foot pedals, stood on by straw-hatted, gray-bearded Mr. McHenry, and towing a tall red box covered by a plastic parasol lid—until you turn a yellow knob and Zebedee pops up, with ketchup-red head, white eyes, black topknot, black horns or whiskers, blue hands—well, it could be anything from a mammal to an insect. The back of the model's box lists a number of other items that link this item with the Magic Roundabout Car, including eight individual figures (861 Florence, 862 Zebedee—as if one weren't enough!—863 Mr. Rusty, 865 Basil, 868 Dylan the Rabbit, 806 Dougal, 864 Brian the Snail and 866 Ermintrude the Cow—sorry, but that's the order they're listed in), 851 Magic Roundabout Train, 852 Magic Roundabout Musical Carousel and 853 Magic Roundabout Playground, in addition to 807. They seem to have come out in 1972 or '73 and to have been sold only in Britain.

150: Surtees TS9B Formula I, 116 mm, first of the new 1/36 racers, in the blue and white of the Brooke Bond Oxo/Rob Walker team, with black engine and air box, chromed exhausts and labels aplenty; through 1964, also appearing in purple and white and, in a gift set, blue and yellow.

151: McLaren M19A, 112 mm, in the white, orange and black of Yardley, with the usual details and a highly unlikely racing number "55;" through 1977.

153: Surtees TS9B again, 112 mm, with different bodywork in the red-white-green colors of Ceramic Pagnossin, plus the usual details; through 1973.

308: Monte Carlo Mini-Cooper, 73 mm, in yellow with license plates, racing number "177" and rally emblems—the front one on the sump guard—plus the roof rack with two spare wheels formerly seen on 339; through 1976.

811: James Bond's Moon Buggy, 113 mm, an awful contraption with white body, blue chassis, red equipment, fat yellow tires and an American flag. (Funny, I thought James Bond was British.) Made in small quantities through 1973 and quite rare now.

1973: ONE THIRTY-SIXTH

As the Grand Prix cars of 1972 had suggested, 1/36 scale was the coming thing for Corgi, as it was for Dinky at the same time. 1973 brought a wholesale shift to the larger scale, with the result that the new models looked out of place beside the older ones. Since many collectors are 1/43 oriented, it was only natural that collector interest should fall off at this point, with some simply refusing to add the 1/36 scale models to their collections, while others collect them as before but bemoan the larger scale—and prices to match. The 1973 issues were:

167: USA Racing Buggy, 95 mm, an odd collection of bars and slabs holding two men and a rear engine, with a spare knobby tire on the roof and labels with alarming patterns of stars and stripes; produced through 1974, resurrected in 1979 and modified to become the Penguinmobile.

169: Starfighter Silver Streak Swedish Jet Dragster, 155 mm, a chrome-plated jet engine on wheels, with a driver in its blue and orange nose cone; made through 1965 and revived in 1979 as Captain America's Jetmobile.

170: Radio Luxembourg Dragster, 146 mm, a blue and yellow Quartermaster with new labels (John Woolfe Racing; driver Dennis Priddle); through 1976.

329: 1965 Mustang Mach I Rally Car, 113 mm, a revised 391 in dark green with multicolored labels and white base; through 1976.

392: Bertone Shake Buggy, 89 mm, a red or green beach buggy with a touch of class, a green interior, white base, chrome engine and glorified roll bar, and a hood decal based loosely on the Italian flag; through 1974.

394: Datsun 240Z East African Safari, 97 mm, originally red and black, then all red, with opening doors, racing labels and spoked wheels; through 1976.

396: Datsun 240Z Rally Car, 97 mm, the same car in red and white with different labels including number "46" (394 is number "11"); also through 1976.

402: Ford Cortina GXL Police Car, 102 mm, in white with stripes, roof sign, dome light and a siren on the front bumper that looks like a battering ram; through 1977.

152: Ferrari 312B2 Formula I, 104 mm, in red and white with the usual details and decals; through 1975.

154: Lotus JPS Formula I, 130 mm, in John Player black and gold; still in production, though John Player no longer sponsors Team Lotus.

459: Raygo Rascal 400 Roller, 125 mm, a massive dark yellow machine with silver roller, green engine (no kidding) and chromed parts; through 1978.

900: Tiger Tank, 103 mm, first in a series of military models made for Corgi in Hong Kong, excellently detailed, in tan and green camouflage; through 1978.

901: Centurion Tank, 121 mm, another fine model in darker camouflage (more green, less tan); both have an unusual-looking but very effective type of plastic treads; through 1978.

1154: Mack Priestman Crane Truck, 240 mm, a red Mack long-nose chassis-cab unit with a crane much like the 1153 shovel; through 1976.

GS 19: Land Rover and Airplane on Trailer, the plane having demountable wings and canopy so as to fit on a long narrow two-wheel trailer; through 1977.

1974: A DASTARDLY THING

In 1974 the change to 1/36 scale continued, with one model actually produced in 1/18 scale. New racing and sports cars, commercials, tractors, tanks and gift sets were produced, a series of futuristic "Hi-Speed" vehicles was born, and Dick Dastardly joined the Corgi family. The new models were:

324: 1973 Ferrari Daytona Le-Mans, 122 mm, the same car in dark yellow with red-white-black "JCB" and "Anthony Bamford" racing labels, representing a Corgi-sponsored Le Mans participant of 1973; apparently issued only in 1974 and not too common.

331: Ford Capri GT Rally, 102 mm, in white and black with "Texaco" labels, a revision of the earlier 303 and 311; through 1976.

1102: Berliet-Fruehauf Bottom Dumper, 287 mm, a yellow and orange bulk-carrier semi pulled by a yellow Berliet cab with black chassis and exhaust; through 1977.

1104: Race Horse Transporter, 256 mm, a green and orange Bedford semi-trailer truck with opening stalls, four blanketed horses and a stableboy; replaced by 1105 in 1977.

50: Massey-Ferguson 50-B Tractor, 98 mm, a modern closed-cab machine in dark yellow; through 1977.

54: Massey-Ferguson 50-B Tractor with Shovel, 150 mm, the same tractor in the same color, equipped with a front loader; still in production.

155: Shadow DN1 Formula I, 132 mm, a not overly detailed model in UOP black, with Jackie Oliver driving; produced through 1976.

156: Shadow DN1, again, this time in white and red Embassy Racing colors with Graham Hill at the wheel; also made through 1976.

159: Indianapolis STP Eagle, 132 mm, a red number "20" with appropriate labels, engine detail including a turbocharger, and Gordon Johncock driving; through 1976.

190: Lotus JPS Formula I, like 154 but twice as big, in 1/18 scale, with wheels that can be taken off (no, not Golden Jacks!); through 1977.

319: Lamborghini Miura, 95 mm, a 1/43 scale leftover modified from 342, now in silver with purple and yellow stripes, racing numbers and Whizzwheels) through 1975.

323: Ferrari Daytona, 122 mm, back to 1/36 scale with this white competition coupe with red and blue trim, opening doors, tinted glass and racing labels; through 1978.

397: Porsche-Audi 917-10, 120 mm, a great flat model of a Can-Am sports-racer, originally white, later orange; produced through 1978, then used for Captain Marvel's car the following year.

400: Volkswagen Driving School Car, 92 mm, in red or blue with "Corgi Motor School" labels and a huge steering wheel on the roof that steers the car as the roof signs of the old driving school Austins did; modified and renumbered 401 in 1976.

403: Thwaites Tusker Skip Dumper, 83 mm, a jaunty yellow thing with tipper in front, driver and motor side by side behind it; through 1979.

700: Motorway Service Ambulance, 98 mm, first of the futuristic Hi-Speed models, in white with blue dome light and windows plus appropriate labels; through 1979.

701: Inter-City Mini-Bus, 107 mm, an impossibly low, wide orange creation with too much clear window space, including part of the roof, and a single door at the rear; through 1978.

809: Dick Dastardly's Racing Car, 128 mm, a horrid blue and yellow racer with big red wheels, driven by fiendish Dick, with his faithful green (yes, green) Muttley crouched atop the engine facing aft; produced only in 1974, it seems, though it is not at all rare.

902: M60 A1 Tank, 115 mm, in tan-green-gray camouflage, with the fine detail typical of the tank series; still in production.

903: Chieftain Tank, 130 mm, a big bruiser in a grim shade of dark olive, with the usual details; still in production.

GS 4: Massey-Ferguson Tractor (50) and a hay trailer complete with a load of plastic hay (not available separately); through 1975.

GS 10: Centurion Tank (901) and Transporter; through 1978.

The 1974 catalog also shows sixteen diecast airplanes, numbered 1301 through 1317, with no 1314. One of them appeared again in 1979; beyond this I know nothing of their history.

1975: MINISSIMA AND ROUTEMASTER

Another year of few new issues followed. In 1975, the 920 series of helicopters began, but the most interesting models issued then were probably the little Minissima and the big new version of the Routemaster doubledecker bus. The new issues for 1975 were:

285: Mercedes-Benz 240D, 127 mm, in silver or metallic blue, with opening front doors, trailer hitch, and a new Whizzwheel design; still in production.

286: Jaguar XJC V-12, 127 mm, in red, blue or gold, with black roof, opening doors and hood, trailer hitch and the same wheel type as the Mercedes; through 1979.

469: Leyland London Routemaster Bus, 123 mm, larger successor to 468 but still in London Transport red, with "BTA Welcome to Britain" labels; promotional issues include a red Design Center and an orange Cadbury's of 1979; still in production, and used for the 471 Silver Jubilee version in 1977.

1103: Pathfinder Airport Crash Truck, 240 mm, a monster in red and silver, with an operating water cannon (one squeezes a bag at the other end of the hose) and electronic battery-operated siren; still in production.

1144: Berliet Wrecker, 130 mm, the red long-nose Berliet cab with rear body and twin booms much like those of the 1142 Holmes Wrecker; through 1978.

158: Tyrrell-Elf Formula I, 110 mm, the dark-blue four-wheel 006/2 with "Elf" labels, as driven by Jackie Stewart; produced through 1978.

287: Citroen Dyane, 115 mm, in yellow with black roof, opening rear hatch, the same type of wheels again, and labels showing a comic duck who seems to think he's Napoleon; through 1978.

288: Minissima, 63 mm, a sort of cube on wheels with a slanting front, rear door, black interior and stripe between its cream top and light green bottom; through 1979.

482: Range Rover Ambulance, 100 mm, much like the 461 police version, still in white but with blue dome lights, red cross and "Ambulance" labels and a stretcher with two bearers; through 1977.

702: Breakdown Truck, 100 mm, the third Hi-Speed vehicle, a squatty red wrecker with the same nose as the ambulance and a silly black boom and gold hook; through 1979.

904: King Tiger Tank, 120 mm, in orange and tan camouflage with the usual details; through 1978.

905: SU-100 Tank Destroyer, 101 mm, in white and gray camouflage, with Russian red stars and an olive commander who pops up in his turret at the push of a red lever in the rear (the tank's rear, not his); through 1977.

906: Saladin Armored Car, 90 mm, a fine model in olive, reminiscent of Dinky military models of bygone days; through 1977.

920: Bell AH-1G Army Helicopter, 130 mm, in tan and olive camouflage with two-blade rotor and skid landing gear; still in production.

921: Hughes OH-6A Police Helicopter, 143 mm, in white with police labels and stripes, four-blade rotor and skids, a fatter-bodied machine than 920; still in production.

1155: Skyscraper Tower Crane, 340 mm high, a huge model with red cab, black treads on yellow hubs and yellow vertical tower with horizontal boom at the top; through 1979.

GS 29: Ferrari Daytona with Formula I Surtees on trailer (323 and 150), both in Duckhams blue and yellow; through 1976.

1976: MAZDA, MINI AND KOJAK

More new Corgis appeared in 1976 than had in any year since 1970, and they included a bit of almost everything: a new Mini, a VW Polo and several other cars, three versions of a Mazda pickup truck, Corgi's first caravan trailer and a new TV-hero model, Kojak's Buick. The new issues were:

290: Kojak's 1976 Buick Century Police Car, 150 mm, a vast metallic brown car with red light on the left side, Sgt. Crocker shooting from the back seat and Kojak pursuing the bad guys on foot; still in production.

315: Lotus Elite, 120 mm, in light red with black grille, bumpers and base (or black and gold in a gift set) and opening doors; changed to 301, another competition model, in 1979.

384: Volkswagen 1200 Rally Car, 92 mm, the 383 Beetle in bright blue with number "5" and stripes; through 1977.

401: Volkswagen 1200 Driving School Car, 92 mm, still in metallic blue with rooftop steering wheel and only minor changes from 400; through 1977.

1157: Ford Esso Tanker, 270 mm, the white and red Esso semi-trailer unit from 1152, pulled by a new white Ford tilt-cab tractor; current. 1158: Ford Exxon Tanker; 1976 only. 1159: Ford Car Transport; through 1979.

1160: Ford Gulf Tanker, 270 mm, the same white cab with a blue tanker semi bearing an orange, blue and white Gulf logo; through 1978.

160: Hesketh Formula I, 130 mm, in white with stripes, names (the driver is just plain "James"), numbers, etc.; produced through 1978.

191: McLaren Formula I, 245 mm, in white and red with plenty of details, a 1/18 scale companion to the 190 Lotus; still in production.

200: Mini 1000, 85 mm, almost as large as life, in blue with red-white-blue roof label that looks suspiciously like a piece of a Union Jack! Made through 1978, then replaced by the 201 competition model.

289: VW Polo, 97 mm, in light green with opening doors and hatchback, still in production, accompanied by 2894, a German mail car in yellow, and appearing in 1979 as the 302 competition version as well.

314: Fiat X1-9 Coupe, 110 mm, green or silver with black trim and opening doors; produced through 1979, then revised in 1980 as the 306 competition model.

409: Mercedes-Benz Unimog Rear Dumper, 103 mm, in orange and red, yellow and blue or blue and yellow, with a big cab and small quarry-type tipper; through 1977.

411: Mercedes-Benz 240D Taxi, 127 mm, 285 in orange and black, later in cream, with roof sign and labels; still in production.

412: Mercedes-Benz 240D Police Car, 127 mm, in German white and green with blue dome light and "Polizei" labels; also current.

413: Mazda Motorway Maintenance Truck, 120 mm, the first of three Mazda pickup variations of 1976, in yellow with overhead service tower, workman and supplies; through 1978.

414: Jaguar XK12C Coast Guard Car, 127 mm, in white with blue stripe, lettering and a massive signboard-dome light-siren roof attachment; through 1977, turning into the very similar 429 police car the following year.

415: Mazda Pickup with Camper, 140 mm, the same pickup in red with a removable white shell camper; through 1978.

490: Caravan Trailer, 125 mm, white with blue trim and a red and white awning that slides out, Corgi's first and only house trailer; through 1979.

493: Mazda B-1600 Pickup Truck 120 mm, the basic Mazda in blue with dropping tailgate; made through 1978 and customized as 440 in 1979.

703: Hi-Speed Fire Engine, 115 mm, last of the 700 series, a light red combination pumper and ladder truck, too sleek and smooth to look real; through 1978.

907: Halftrack Rocket Launcher, 167 mm, a gray German vehicle that fires the plastic rockets carried in its two-wheel trailer; still in production.

922: Sikorsky Skycrane Casualty Helicopter, 160 mm, with red body, white box below it, and six-blade rotor; through 1978.

925: Batcopter, 143 mm, in black with four-blade batwing rotor in red; in production.

1101: Warner & Swasey Mobile Crane, 155 mm, in yellow with red lettering, black chassis and yellow extending support jacks; in production.

1110: JCB Crawler Loader, 155 mm, a yellow and white front loader on treads, with a red shovel; in production.

GS 5: Massey-Ferguson Tractor (50) and the long low-side trailer last seen with a load of hay, now with livestock and fencing; through 1977.

GS 17: Bell Helicopter, Tiger Tank and Saladin (920, 900 and 906); current.

GS 18: Emergency Set including 402 Police Car, 482 Range Rover Ambulance and 921 Police Helicopter; through 1977, replaced by GS 20 in 1978.

GS 24: Mercedes 240D and Caravan Trailer (285 and 490); current, with new colors in 1980.

GS 28: Mazda Pickup (493) with rubber dinghy on trailer; through 1978.

GS 31: Safari Land Rover and Lion Cage Trailer, both new versions in white with black zebra stripes; current.

GS 32: Lotus Elite and Lotus Formula I on trailer (315 and 154), both in John Player black and gold; current.

1977: JAMES BOND AND SIMON SNORKEL

In 1977 Corgi celebrated Queen Elizabeth's Silver Jubilee with a horsedrawn State Landau and a silver version of the Routemaster Bus, and followed their usual inclinations with a James Bond Lotus Esprit, Starsky and Hutch Ford Torino, Tarzan and Batman sets, and even a colorful open-top Disneyland Bus—alas, not for sale in the USA. There were new military, police and security vehicles too, not to mention a revised Simon Snorkel fire truck, among the 1977 Corgi Toys:

470: Leyland Disneyland Bus, 123 mm, a Routemaster minus its roof, in yellow with Disneyland logo and red seats; through 1978 and not sold in the USA.

471: Leyland Silver Jubilee Bus, 123 mm, the whole Routemaster in silver with "Woolworth Welcomes the World" logo, Union Jacks and such; issued only in 1977.

1105: Berliet Racehorse Transporter, 280 mm, in golden brown and white, with ramps and horses, replacing the earlier 1104; current.

1112: David Brown Combine Harvester, 220 mm, in red, white and black, not a separate vehicle like old 1111 but attached to the 55 tractor; through 1978.

55: David Brown Tractor, 105 mm, with modern closed cab, in white with red chassis, black roof and stack; still in production.

56: Tipping Farm Trailer, 130 mm, in red and either yellow or white; also current.

161: Tyrrell Formula I, 113 mm, the six-wheeler in blue and white; revised and renumbered 162 the following year.

269: James Bond's Lotus Esprit, 120 mm, flat and white, "ingeniously equipped for underwater missions with extending hydroplanes, concealed fins and a remote-controlled battery of rockets;" current.

291: AMC Pacer, 118 mm, with bulbous metallic maroon body and cream interior, made in this form through 1978 and revised in that year into the 484 Rescue Car.

292: Starsky and Hutch's Ford Torino, 153 mm, in red and white with figures of the two policemen and a suspect; current.

293: Renault 5 TS, 97 mm, in gold with black trim and opening doors; current, with an Alpine version, 294, forthcoming in 1980.

416: Buick Century Police Car, 150 mm, Kojak's car now in metallic blue with white "Police" lettering; through 1978, since then, as 260, representing the City of Metropolis.

421: Forest Warden Land Rover, 135 mm, in red-orange with white roof rack, already used in one set and destined for use in several others; through 1978. The 1977 catalog shows it in plain gold with black rack and no labels.

422: Riot Police Armored Car, 95 mm, in white and red, with roof spotlight and two swiveling water cannons; current.

424: Security Van, 100 mm, the 700 Ambulance casting in black with baby blue plastic window bars and front bumpers, yellow base and "Security" lettering, a very unconvincing model; through 1979.

489: VW Polo Police Car, 97 mm, in white and green with "Polizei" lettering, as well as 4894, the same car in yellow and white as an A.D.A.C. service car; current.

908: AMX Recovery Tank, 127 mm, in olive with crane and winch, dozer blade, spare gun barrel, trestles and figures; current.

909: Quad Gun Tractor with Field Gun and Ammo Trailer, 280 mm, in golden tan; current.

924: Air-Sea Rescue Helicopter, 150 mm, in blue with yellow pontoons and black four-blade rotor, or orange with black pontoons and yellow rotor; current.

1126: Simon Snorkel Fire Engine, 265 mm, a new version in red with white arm and yellow basket and jacks; current.

1156: Volvo Concrete Mixer, 195 mm, in yellow, red and orange, with mixer drum that can be made to rotate as the vehicle moves; current.

GS 34: David Brown Tractor and Tipping Trailer (55 and 56); through 1979.

GS 36: Tarzan Set, with Land Rover, animal trailer, rubber dinghy and its trailer, and two- and four-footed creatures; through 1978.

GS 37: Fiat X1-9 and Powerboat, a racing craft with Carlsberg labels; current.

GS 38: Mini Camping Set, the 200 Mini with plastic tent, campers and barbecue; through 1978.

GS 40: Batmobile, Batboat and Batcopter (267, 107 and 925); current.

GS 41: Silver Jubilee State Landau, 300 mm, magnificent in red with lavish trim, pulled by four white horses and bearing Her Majesty and His Royal Highness; current.

1978: THE YEAR OF THE VAN

While 1978 brought new Corgis of many kinds, from a Batbike to a Human Cannonball circus truck, from new cars for James Bond and the Saint to a new London Taxi, it was above all the year of the Chevrolet Van. Private owners, Charlie's Angels, Coca-Cola, Superman and the circus all had their own vans. The new issues were:

1161: Ford Aral Tank Truck, 270 mm, in Aral blue and white, for the German market; current.

1163: Human Cannonball Truck, with Berliet cab, in red, yellow and blue Jean Richard Circus colors, with silver-suited man to be fired from the cannon; current.

162: Tyrrell P34 Formula I, 113 mm, slightly changed from the previous year's 161, in blue and white; through 1979.

268: Batbike, 110 mm, a black motorcycle with red trim and wings, Batman in blue or mauve, and two rocket launchers; current.

271: James Bond's Aston Martin, 130 mm, the third version of this modern-day classic toy, in silver gray with the expected surprises; current.

319: Jaguar XJS, 128 mm, in metallic maroon with black trim, opening doors and a new Whizzwheel pattern; current, and put to specialized use as well.

320: The Saint's Jaguar XJS, 128 mm, the same car in white with Simon Templar's symbol on the hood; current.

321: Porsche 924, 118 mm, in metallic light brown with opening doors and rear hatch; current, also used in police and competition forms (430 and 303).

405: Chevrolet Superior Ambulance, 119 mm, a van-type in white with orange roof, red dome light and labels, attendant and patient; current.

419: Covered Jeep, 100 mm, a metallic green CJ-5 with removable white plastic top, white wheels and knobby tires; through 1979, when it became the 441 Golden Eagle.

423: Rough Rider Van, 122 mm, first of the private-owner Chevy vans, in yellow with huge labels showing a motorcyclist; 1978 only.

425: London Taxi, 121 mm, a new version of the classic Austin in the usual black; current.

426: Circus Booking Office, 122 mm, the Chevy Van in yellow with red canopy and roof rack, blue loudspeakers and Pinder-Jean Richard logo; current.

428: Renault 5 Police Car, 97 mm, 293 in white and black, with blue dome light and white lettering; through 1979.

429: Jaguar XJ12C Police Car, 127 mm, in white with stripes, dome light and roof sign, a new use for the phased-out Coast Guard car; current.

430: Porsche 924 Police Car, 118 mm, 321 in German white and green with "Polizei" labels; current.

431: Vanatic, 122 mm, the Chevy Van in white with its name and other labels; current.

432: Vantastic, 122 mm, this time in black with its own labels; current.

433: Van-ishing Point, 122 mm, the same again in gold—but it seems to have lived up to its name and vanished before getting into production.

434: Charlie's Angels' Van, 122 mm, this time in pink with labels showing three lethal ladies in silhouette; current.

435: Super Van, 122 mm, in silver with logo showing Superman in action; current.

437: Coca-Cola Van, 122 mm, in red with white stripe and Coca-Cola logo; current.

484: AMC Pacer Rescue Car, 118 mm, in white with black hood, orange rear, red dome lights and "Rescue" lettering, based on 291; current.

9212 and 9921: Netherlands and German Police Helicopters, 143 mm, both white with varying labels and twelve-bladed rotors; probably current in Holland and Germany.

926: Stromberg's Jet Ranger Helicopter, 156 mm, in black with yellow trim and rockets to fire at James Bond; through 1979.

927: Chopper Squad Surf Rescue Helicopter, 156 mm, the same Jet Ranger in blue and white; through 1979.

1113: Hyster Stacatruck, 212 mm, a yellow and black fork-lift truck that does what you'd expect it to; current.

GS 20: Emergency Set: 429 Jaguar Police Car, 482 Range Rover Ambulance, and 921 Police Helicopter, plus signs and figures; current.

GS 35: Chopper Squad Rescue Set, with 927 Helicopter, open blue Jeep and Surf Rescue boat on trailer; through 1979.

GS 42: Agricultural Set: 55 Tractor, 56 Trailer, plus plastic silo and grain elevator conveyor belt; current.

GS 44: Police Land Rover and Horse Trailer, in white with labels, plus policeman on horse; current.

GS 45: RCMP Land Rover and Horse Trailer, the same models in blue and white Royal Canadian Mounted Police colors; current.

GS 47: Pony Club Land Rover and Horse Trailer, the same theme again in brown and white for the private sector; current.

GS 48: Jean Richard Circus Set, with booking office van, open trailer, Land Rover and cage trailer, Human Cannonball Truck, tent, ring and figures; current.

GS 49: Flying Club Set, a revised GS 19 with green and white Jeep pulling the trailer with the airplane on it; current.

1979: THE COMIC-STRIP HEROES

With few exceptions, the new Corgis of 1979 were populated by comic-strip, TV and movie heroes and villains in vast numbers. The few exceptions included several revisions of existing models plus a very few new cars and trucks:

201: Mini 1000 Competition Car, 85 mm, 200 in silver with racing labels; in production as of 1980, as are all other 1979 issues unless otherwise noted.

259: Penguinmobile, 95 mm, a white adaptation of the 167 Racing Buggy, with its driver under a red and yellow parasol.

260: Metropolis Police Car, 150 mm, 416 in blue again with the emblem of Superman's home town.

261: Spiderbuggy, 150 mm, a red and blue open Jeep with Spiderman at the wheel and the Green Goblin in a plastic bag hanging from a boom in the back.

262: Captain Marvel's Porsche, 120 mm, 397 in white with Captain Marvel driving and multi-colored labels.

263: Captain America Jetmobile, 155 mm, the 169 dragster in red, white and blue.

264: The Incredible Hulk, 120 mm, the Mazda pickup truck with a cage in back from which the great one emerges.

265: Supermobile, 148 mm, an indescribable blue craft with silver "striking fist action" arms.

266: Spiderbike, 115 mm, a black and red motorcycle, with Spiderman and his webs.

279: Rolls-Royce Corniche, 144 mm, in metallic maroon, with opening hood, trunk and doors, detailed engine and tilting seat backs.

300: Ferrari Daytona, 120 mm, a competition 323 in green with racing labels.

301: Lotus Elite, 120 mm, a yellow racing version of 315, with labels.

302: VW Polo, 97 mm, 289 in metallic brown competition form, plus labels.

325: Chevrolet Caprice, 150 mm, in light metallic green; apparently issued only in 1979, used in police and taxi forms (326 and 327) in 1980.

4303: Porsche Police Car, 118 mm, this time in white and black with "Police" labels.

440: Mazda Custom Pickup Truck, 120 mm, 493 in yellow with multicolored labels.

441: Golden Eagle Jeep, 100 mm, 419 in golden brown with yellow plastic top, plus labels.

928: Spidercopter, 142 mm, in blue with red tongue that flicks out, red spider legs and spiderweb rotor.

929: Daily Planet Helicopter, 156 mm, in red and white, another version of the Jet Ranger, this time for reporters who follow Superman.

1107: Berliet Container Truck, 290 mm, with blue and white cab and flat semi-trailer carrying two gray United States Lines containers. Not in the 1980 catalog—was it issued?

1109: Michelin Truck, 243 mm, with blue Ford cab and low-side semi-trailer, two yellow plastic covers with blue Michelin logo, and a white tire-man perched atop the cab.

1116: Refuse Collector Truck, 151 mm, with orange chassis and cab and silver rear body, hinged tail and rotating bar, plus labels.

1315, 1320 and 1325: Boeing 747 (shown in the 1974 catalog), Vickers VC-10 and Douglas DC-10 (both apparently newer than 1974).

2022, 2023, 2024 and 2026: X-ploratrons, four fantastic twenty-first-century vehicles for exploring other planets.

2030 through 2033: The Muppets: Kermit's Kar in yellow, Fozzie Bear's truck in red and blue, Miss Piggy's Sports Coupe in pink and Animal's Percussionmobile in orange.

GS 30: Circus Land Rover and Animal Trailer, two pieces from the bigger GS 48.

GS 43: Farm Silo and Elevator, two pieces from GS 42.

1980: INTO THE TWENTY-FIRST CENTURY

We cannot say at this time whether all the new models shown in the 1980 Corgi catalog will actually materialize, or whether the colors and details will be as shown. As they stand in print, they show a continuation of present-day trends: superheroes and spacecraft, police and firefighting vehicles, competition sports cars and the like:

294: Renault 5 Alpine, 97 mm, a special version of 293.

303: Porsche 924, 118 mm, a racing version of 321, apparently in gold with labels.

306: Fiat X1-9, 110 mm, 314 in competition form, blue with labels.

326: Chevrolet Caprice Police Car, 150 mm, the previous year's 325 in black and white.

327: Chevrolet Caprice Taxi, 150 mm, the same car in yellow with roof sign.

329: Opel Senator, 142 mm, in gold with opening doors (put to special use as 332).

332: Opel Doctor's Emergency Car, 142 mm, in white and red "Notarzt" form.

334: Ford's New Trendsetter for the '80's: "Full details to await launch."

338: Rover 3500, 140 mm, in blue with opening doors, hood and hatchback plus hinged parcel shelf (also used as 339).

339: Rover 3500 Police Car, 140 mm, in white with dome light, roof sign and labels.

342: The Professionals Ford Capri, 124 mm, a silver coupe with opening hood and trunk, plus figures of three crime-fighters.

343: Ford Capri 3-Liter S, 124 mm, the same 343 in the same color, without the cops.

348: Vega$ Ford Thunderbird, 124 mm, a red '50's convertible with Dan Tanner driving.

406: Mercedes-Benz Bonna Ambulance, 150 mm, in cream with red labels and blue dome lights, stretcher, bearers and patient.

647: Buck Rogers Starfighter, 150 mm, a white and blue spacecraft with swing wings and rocket launchers, for Buck to use "in the 25th Century."

648: NASA Space Shuttle, 156 mm, in white with opening hatches and satellite.

649: James Bond's Space Shuttle, 156 mm, the same craft with different labels.

930: Drax Airlines Helicopter, 156 mm, another Jet Ranger, complete with rockets, in white, orange and yellow.

931: Jet Ranger Police Helicopter, 156 mm, this time in white and red with rescue winch.

1001: HCB-Angus Firestreak Firefighter, 165 mm, a big red van with firefighting and rescue equipment and two figures.

1117: Mercedes-Faun Street Sweeper, 135 mm, in orange with red and white stripes, rotating brushes, "gulley syphon" and operator.

1164: Dolphinarium Truck, 290 mm, a blue Berliet semi-trailer truck with a tank that can be filled with water, plus figures including a dolphin jumping through a hoop.

GS 2: Construction Set: 54 Tractor with Shovel, 440 Mazda Pickup and, in the Mazda, a cement mixer that used to be a Corgi Junior model.

GS 11: London Set: a new version of the traditional theme, with 425 London Taxi, 469 Routemaster Bus, and the mounted policeman from GS 44.

GS 19: Emergency Set: 339 Rover Police Car, 931 Jet Ranger Helicopter, policeman and signs.

GS 21: Superman Set: 265 Supermobile, 260 Police Car and 929 Daily Planet Helicopter.

GS 22: James Bond Set: 269 Lotus, 271 Aston Martin and 649 Space Shuttle.

GS 23: Spiderman Set: 261 Spiderbuggy, 266 Spiderbike and 928 Spidercopter.

GS 25: Matra Rancho and Motorcycle Trailer, both completely new. We assume the Rancho, at least, will subsequently be issued separately.

GS 38: Powerboat Team, the 319 Jaguar in white and red, pulling a trailer with a red racing boat like that of GS 37.

AFTERWORD—CORGI'S SILVER JUBILEE

Here we have seen twenty-five years of Corgi production. The firm's great rival, Dinky, is succumbing to financial difficulties, but Corgi goes on producing toys that, while some of them may not appeal to serious collectors, certainly seem to be what the general public wants. We hobbyists must accept the fact that firms like Corgi are in business to sell toys to the public, and that we constitute a very small percentage of their market, too small to have any significant effect on what they produce. We assume the Corgi story will continue far into the future, with new surprises and frequent innovations awaiting the customer as before.

For the collector, though, it is naturally the earlier models that are of the greatest interest, and we have tried to stress them here. We could have added much more data, but this book would then have been larger, much more costly, and less interesting to the public. The collector is referred to the *Corgi Checklist* published in 1977 by Ron Meyer of British Columbia, the articles on 1956-65 Corgi Toys by Tony Gleave in the British magazine, *Modeller's World*, and to other articles and lists in print for more specific information on Corgis.

Not included in this text are: Trophy Models (a few early Corgis in gold-plated finish with sheet metal baseplates), Corgi Cubs (recent low-fidelity toy vehicles, but hardly models), Corgi Junior models, Corgi Rockets and their Husky predecessors (which would require a volume all their own), and various minor accessories, spare parts, and so on.

We hope you have found this book interesting and informative, and would be happy to hear your comments.

James Wieland   Dr. Edward Force
E2 Tapping Reeve   42 Warham Street
Litchfield, Connecticut 06759   Windsor, Connecticut 06095

Notes

Many names in this listing are given in incomplete form for the sake of brevity. See the text for the full and exact names of the models.

Numbers ending on -A or -S are not included in this list. See the text for the years 1959-1963 for these revision numbers, or see the listing of the original model in the text.

The numbers of the Explorations and the Muppets models are those of the larger Corgi Junior vehicles, but the models are not shown in the Corgi Junior sections of the Corgi catalogs, and they seem to fit in better with the large-scale Corgi Toys anyway, so we have included them here.

A date of issue followed by a hyphen and no date of withdrawal indicates that the model is still in production as of 1980. The date of issue of a model is basically that of its first appearance in a Corgi catalog. It is quite possible that some models were actually put on the market late in the year previous to their first catalog appearance. In addition, some models made for specific markets were not always shown in the catalogs. Examples of these are the police cars and other service vehicles made for specific European countries. The Magic Roundabout toys were apparently sold only in Britain. For the aircraft in the 1300 series, we know neither the date of issue nor that of withdrawal.

Colors of models listed in the text are taken chiefly from Tony Gleave's articles and Ron Meyer's checklist. It is possible that two colors listed for a model may be two individuals' efforts to describe the same color.

Automotive library additions

Fearsome Fords 1959-1973. Over 250 photos of these great cars accompany 182 pages of interesting information. Softbound, large format.

Corvair Affair. The whole Corvair story including styling, mechanicals and the Nader connection. 176 pages, over 140 great illustrations.

Motoring Mascots of the World. Lavish collection of hood mascots accompanied by informative text. 196 pages, 802 illustrations.

Classic Motorbooks Chevy El Camino 1959-1982 Photofacts. 80 pages packed full of info on these car/trucks. Softbound, about 200 photos.

Classic Motorbooks Chrysler 300 1955-1961 Photofacts. Over 125 photos accompany lots of info on these cars. Softbound, 80 pages.

Classic Motorbooks Pontiac Trans Am 1969-1973 Photofacts. Over 125 great photos help tell the story. 80 pages, softbound.

Illustrated Porsche Buyer's Guide. Covers the 356 through the 944 from 1950 to 1983 with lots of photos. Softbound, 175 pages.

Ferraris For The Road. Provides lavish pictorial coverage of Ferrari production models. In the Survivors Series. 126 pages, 269 photos, many in color.

Tootsietoys: World's First Diecast Models. Great reference source; over 360 models shown, with informative historical text. 100 pages, softbound.

American Car Spotter's Guide 1940-1965. Covers 66 makes—almost 3,000 illustrations. 358 pages, softbound.

American Car Spotter's Guide 1966-1980. Giant pictorial source with over 3,600 illustrations. 432 pages, softbound.

The Production Figure Book For U.S. Cars. Reflects the relative rarity of various makes, models, body styles, etc. Softbound, 180 pages.

American Truck Spotter's Guide 1920-1970. 170 makes are covered with over 2,000 illustrations. Softbound, 330 pages.

Pickup and Van Spotter's Guide 1945-1982. Covers 15 U.S. and foreign makes with over 1,200 illustrations, 160 pages, softbound.

The Big "Little GTO" Book. All of these Great Ones by Pontiac are covered—1965-1974. Over 150 great photos, 235 pages. Large format, softbound.

Chevy Super Sports 1961-1976. Exciting story of these hot cars with complete specs and data. 176 pages, 234 illustrations, softbound. Large format.

Son of Muscle Car Mania. 176 pages of more great ads from the 1962-1974 muscle car era. All U.S. makes represented. Softbound, 250 illustrations.

Muscle Car Mania. A collection of advertisements for muscle cars 1964 through 1974. 176 pages, 250 illustrations, softbound.

Motorbooks International
Publishers & Wholesalers Inc.
Osceola, Wisconsin 54020, USA